The Dialogue Between Science and Religion
Challenges and Future Directions

Antje Jackelén

The Dialogue Between Science and Religion
Challenges and Future Directions

Proceedings of the Third Annual Goshen Conference on Religion and Science

Antje Jackelén
Zygon Center for Religion and Science
and
Lutheran School of Theology at Chicago

Edited by: Carl S. Helrich
Goshen College

Library and Archives Canada Cataloguing in Publication

Goshen Conference on Religion and Science
(3rd : 2003 : Goshen, Ind.)
   The dialogue between science and religion : challenges and future directions : proceedings of the Third Annual Goshen Conference on Religion and Science / Antje Jackelén ; edited by Carl S. Helrich.

Includes index.
ISBN 1-894710-45-2

   1. Religion and science--Congresses. I. Jackelén, Antje II. Helrich, Carl S. III. Title.

BL241.G68 2003   261.5'5   C2004-903244-5

All Bible quotations are used by permission, all rights reserved, and unless otherwise indicated are from the *New Revised Standard Version Bible*, copyright 1989, by the Division of Christian Education of the National Council of the Churches of Christ in the USA; REB, from the *Revised English Bible*; KJV, from the King James Version of The Bible.

THE DIALOGUE BETWEEN RELIGION AND SCIENCE: CHALLENGES AND FUTURE DIRECTIONS

   Copyright©2004 by Pandora Press
   33 Kent Avenue
   Kitchener, Ontario N2G 3R2
   www.pandorapress.com
   All rights reserved

   International Standard Book Number: 1-894710-45-2
   Book and cover design by Cliff Snyder

13 12 11 10 09 08 07 06 05 04   12 11 10 9 8 7 6 5 4 3 2 1

Table of Contents

EDITOR'S PREFACE 7

LECTURES 13

The Challenge of Hermeneutics 15
Antioch and Alexandria:
    The Beginnings of Christian Hermeneutics 16
Hermeneutics in the 20th century 19
Hermeneutics in religion-and-science 21

The Challenge from Feminisms 35
Feminine Imagery in the History of Science 35
Feminist Critique of Science 39
Hermeneutical and Feminist Suspicion Cultivated:
    Creation and Complexity 48

The Challenge from Postmodernisms 54
Nietzsche and Perspectivism 54
The Death of God and Science 59
From Nietzsche to Postmodernism 63
Constructive Postmodernism 64
Looking into the Future of the religion-and-science dialogue .. 72

Sunday Worship 76
Minding God and the Mind and Heart of God 76

DISCUSSIONS 83

Development of Science 85
Muslims 85
Western Christianity 88
Progress in Science and in Religion 89

Time and Eternity 92
Doctoral Dissertation 92
Purgatory and Mansions 95
Christology 98
City of God 98

Language 100
Language and Mathematics 100
Complexity and Chaos 101

Feminism 104
Gender and Science 104
Women in Science 105
Women and Male Images 106
Women and Competition 109

Postmodernism 112
Defined 112
Truth and Judgment 113
Present and Future 115
Hermeneutics 116
Eastern Orthodoxy 119
Epistemology and Brain Science 121
Theologians 124

INDEX 127

NOTES 131

Editor's Preface

The Goshen Conference on Religion and Science is intended to be a forum in which conference participants have an opportunity for close interaction with a thinker and scholar of international stature. The format for the conference was inspired by the very successful Cosmos and Creation conference that convenes at Loyola College in Maryland. There is a single speaker, selected as a person who is an important voice in the religion and science dialog. The speaker presents two public lectures and one internal lecture. There are four discussion sessions. One of these follows the first public lecture and the remaining three take place in more intimate surroundings.

The first Goshen Conference hosted Professor Nancey Murphy of Fuller Theological Seminary as speaker. The second conference hosted Professor George Ellis of the University of Cape Town. Because these two speakers were co-authors of an important contribution to the science and religion dialog,[1] the ideas expressed by both speakers were similar in nature. However, the presentations by Murphy and Ellis were quite different as were the detailed areas covered in each conference.

The third conference hosted Professor Antje Jackelén of the Zygon Center for Religion and Science and the Lutheran School of Theology at Chicago. Professor Jackelén is a systematic theologian whose background includes service as a parish pastor. She was ordained by the Church of Sweden in 1980 and served as a parish pastor for the diocese of Stockholm and the diocese of Lund for 16 years. She also was senior pastor of Gardstanga and served as a pastor at Lund Cathedral.

Professor Jackelén has thought deeply about the three issues she discussed in the lectures, which are important challenges to the religion and science dialog. But then in the third lecture Professor Jackelén admitted that there is really only one issue: hermeneutics. We are confronted finally with the fact that we must convey ideas to one another. And this must be done in the common language of everyday use, even though the concepts we wish to discuss are not those of everyday use. This is a problem that is as old as thought itself and as new as the most modern of sciences.

Of course Professor Jackelén told us where she would take us when we began. But participants did not fully realize the extent of the journey until the conference ended. This has been true of all speakers at the Goshen conference. Each speaker only has a different way of carrying us there.

In each of the lectures Professor Jackelén first gave us some foundation in history. And then moved us fairly rapidly to confront the implications of the subject for the religion and science dialog. But the path she chose in each lecture was not that which one may have anticipated.

In the first lecture she filtered through the ideas of Origen, Gadamer, Newton, Bohr, Heisenberg, and Einstein using her understanding of the difficulty each faced and the crucial role language played in that. In this her audience had to confront the fact that our use of language is important. In the dialog between religion and science, in her words, we have used thick science and thin theology in much of the modern popularized scientific writings, while thick theology is almost unknown to the scientific community. At the same time the understanding of the science that one can gain from the popularized writings is thin. And the theologian is left with thin science and thick theology.

Her understanding of the individual ideas of, for example Bohr and Heisenberg and of Bohr and Einstein was sufficient for her to speak with clarity about some of the deepest scientific debates of the twentieth century. And she addressed the theological positions with authority. The result invites us to acknowledge that the issues are not solely those of expertise. The issues are also in our use of the dirty water and dirty cloths of language, which we must use to get our thoughts, like our dishes, clean.

The scientific community has seen feminism and postmodernism generally as anti-scientific movements. And Professor Jackelén was aware of the possible lack of interest in these topics by the hard scientists present at the conference. But the ideas that she presented and the context in which she placed these ideas were not what one may have expected.

Although she did begin with the ideas of Francis Bacon, she placed feminism and the feminist critique of science as one advocating a becoming rather than a being. This position is characteristic of the modern theories of chaos, nonlinear dynamics and non-equilibrium thermodynamics. This acceptance of a dynamic universe is what she finds in feminist thought.

She then applied these ideas to theology contrasting the idea of a static and simple God to that of a complex God. A plausible counter idea to that of the simple, designing God is of a dynamic God that is more compatible with modern ideas from the sciences.

The challenge to the thinking in theology is then in tune with the challenge to the thinking in the sciences. This is a refreshing position, as well as a sobering position. To her credit, Professor Jackelén does not try to weld science and theology or even social ideas in the way in which the term relativity was once used in the twentieth century, and is still used. The term complexity is no more a blanket than was relativity. Both are scientific terms that must be considered with caution. That complexity and the related concept of emergence have not come to us in the form that the term relativity did in 1905 and in 1915 is indicative of the fact that the issues are not so well-defined at this point.

In the discussions Professor Jackelén provided thorough answers and allowed herself to reflect on what was said and even to explore some ideas on the floor. She has a deep respect for, and understanding of the sciences, even though this is not her primary interest. This was particularly clear in her remarks on dealing with new ideas in the sciences. At one point she remarked on the misunderstanding of relativity that came about because of the common understanding of the word relativity in the English language, and indicated that she wanted to be careful because of this. Although she maintained a similar respect for all the subjects she was more able to engage directly the nuances of theology.

Professor Jackelén provided complete, edited copies of her lectures, with references. David Shumaker helped to prepare these lectures for publication. I would like to acknowledge his efforts with gratitude. His care in matching the final form of these lectures to the requirements of the publisher was appreciated.

In the transcript of the discussions speaker numbers identify participants. Only Antje Jackelén is identified by name. This has been the rule followed in the proceedings of each conference.

These proceedings include a written transcript of the teaching or homily given in the Sunday morning worship service. In the

Editor's Preface

first conference the worship teaching, in the tradition of the Mennonite Church, was presented by a member of the Goshen College faculty, who is an ordained Mennonite pastor, Professor Don Blosser. In the second conference this was presented by Professor Millard Lind, professor emeritus of the Associated Mennonite Biblical Seminaries. In this third conference the teaching should more appropriately be called a homily and was presented by Professor David Hogue of Garrett Evangelical Theological Seminary in Evanston, Illinois.

Carl Helrich
1 January, 2004

Lectures

The principal resource for the conference is the set of lectures presented by the speaker, Professor Antje Jackelén. There are two public lectures and one internal lecture. In addition to conference participants, the public lectures usually draw a small group of people from the Goshen and Elkhart communities. Occasionally groups from neighboring colleges have attended these as well. The public lectures are given on Friday evening and on Saturday morning. The internal lecture, traditionally intended to afford the speaker a more relaxed forum in which to express ideas, is delivered on Sunday morning. All lectures are published here in a final edited form provided by Professor Jackelén, which includes a complete set of notes and abstract of the lectures.

In addition to the lectures presented by the speaker, the homily or message of the Sunday worship is also printed here. Professor David Hogue of Garrett Evangelical Theological Seminary in Evanston, Illinois presented this.

Abstract

This series of three lectures is devoted to an exploration of three challenges for the current dialogue between science and religion: the challenges from hermeneutics, feminisms and postmodernisms.

Hermeneutics, defined as the practice and theory of interpretation and understanding, deals not only with questions of interpreting texts and data: it examines the role and use of language in religion as well as in science, but should not stop there. Results of the post-Kuhnian discussion are used to exemplify a wider range of hermeneutical issues, such as the ideological potential of scientific concepts, the dynamics of interdisciplinarity and the significance of the socio-economic situatedness of science and religion.

Feminist research analyzes the consequences of the interplay of masculine, feminine and gender typologies in religion and science. Examples from the history of science as well as current scientific conceptualizations indicate that beliefs in the inferiority of woman form part of our inherited scientific, religious and metaphysical framework. I will conclude the second lecture with an attempt to apply insights from hermeneutics and feminism to an understanding of creation theology in a scientific perspective.

In the third lecture, I argue that *postmodernism* in its most constructive form shares the best fruits of modernity, especially of the Enlightenment, while at the same time avoiding some of its most serious mistakes. Drawing on the work of Friedrich Nietzsche and his understanding of science, I demonstrate the connection between modern and postmodern, between rationality and piety.

In conclusion, reflecting on the three publics engaged in the dialogue between science and religion—academe, religious communities and societies—I offer an outline of constructive suggestions and critical observations concerning the future of this dialogue.

The Challenge of Hermeneutics

What is hermeneutics? Dictionaries usually tell us something like: "Hermeneutics is the practice and theory of interpretation and understanding." I often say: "Hermeneutics is what turns suspicion from a vice into an art." In other words, hermeneutics is what enables us to find the right balance between skepticism and gullibility. Where the overly skeptical person will miss whatever truth there might be, the excessively trustful person will accept, whatever there might be, as truth. Both lack discernment. They have not understood that thinkers have "a *duty* to be distrustful, to squint out most maliciously from the bottom of every abyss of suspicion," as Friedrich Nietzsche once put it.[1] Hermeneutics claims that the balance between skepticism and gullibility is not just a matter of intuition or taste, but that we can learn to use methods that will allow us to handle the process of understanding and interpreting in rational, intelligible ways. The hermeneutical task starts by taking seriously the critical questions of how we understand and how we interpret. In that sense, hermeneutics is a constructive way of handling the suspicion that we might never get it all right. If we take this seriously, we need to conclude that hermeneutics is not just a name of a couple of methods in the *human* sciences, but it is about the nature of understanding itself. Or, put differently, there is a "hermeneutic fore-structure" preceding all kinds of knowledge.[2]

Before I apply my thesis about the necessity of hermeneutics to the dialogue between science and religion, let us look at the beginnings of hermeneutics to get a clearer sense of where this all comes from in the tradition that has shaped most of us here. As a Christian theologian, I refer to the development of theological hermeneutics.

Antioch and Alexandria: The Beginnings of Christian Hermeneutics

Two ancient cities in the Middle East, Antioch and Alexandria, may be identified as the two places where "the most systematic development of Christian hermeneutics took place."[3] Let us turn to Alexandria first. Clement of Alexandria (d. ca. 214) suggested that since all Scripture speaks in the mysterious language of symbols, allegorical interpretation was required. However, it was not until Origen (185-254) that a more systematic reflection on interpretation was offered. This only happens in the fourth and last part of his *On First Principles*,[4] in the book *On Scripture*.[5] (This book is also called the "first systematic discussion of the hermeneutic problem."[6]) This placement tells us something. It indicates that it is actually Origen's theology (and his fight against the heresies of Marcion and the Valentinian Gnostics) that shapes his method of interpretation.[7] Origen was deeply involved with textual criticism, and worked to prepare a critical and reliable edition of the biblical texts. The *Hexapla* is a product of these ambitions.[8] This shows that the awareness of textual diversity with the impossibility of reconstructing the one true text was already familiar in the early church. The reality of various valid interpretations is by no means a modern discovery.

In spite of Origen's interest in the text itself, his focus is not on literal interpretation but on the disclosure of the text's spiritual sense. He has a sense of the limits of language. In his hermeneutical considerations about an adequate understanding of the Scriptures, he concludes that there are things the significance of which cannot be expressed in words of human language, but rather by mere thought.[9] For Origen, the reason for every misunderstanding of scripture is that scripture is not understood spiritually but according to the letter only: "Now the reason those we have just mentioned have a false understanding of these matters is quite simply that they understand Scripture not according to the spiritual meaning but according to the sound of the letter."[10] Although theoretically Origen distinguished a threefold structure of textual sense—literal, moral and spiritual—in practice (IV 2,4), he distinguished only between 'letter' and 'spirit'. Repeatedly, he acknowledges the need for the interpreter to be guided by the church's rule of faith. Our understanding has to be in compliance with the "regula pietatis,"[11] the rule of piety, or, as we would say today, with the mission statement of the church. Hence, what looks fairly liberal from the outset—non-literal interpretation—is not necessarily liberal at all. It is open to ideological use. There is no reason to become overly optimistic. We are left with a circle, as an Origen scholar points out: "On the one hand, Origen begins with Scripture... On the other hand, Origen approaches Scripture with preconceptions that are in great part determined by his philosophical training and bent of mind."[12]

In Antioch, interpreters used rules built on a tradition different from that of Origen. Here, Christian thinkers followed the tradition of local Jewish exegesis more closely. They "advanced a theory of biblical interpretation which was primarily concerned with literal interpretation, and therefore emphasized textual and grammatical investigation of the Scriptures."[13] Theologians such as Theodore of Mopsuestia[14] (ca. 350-428) saw the dangers of Origen's hermeneutics in the Alexandrian denial of the actual reality of the biblical stories. In a way, there was too much spirituality. Origen's critics were unwilling to lose the historical reality of the biblical revelation in a world of symbols and shadows (Plato!). The Antiochenes were more Aristotelian than Platonist. They rejected a hidden sense of Scripture and assumed that the meanings of the text refer to actual realities "clear and intelligible for every reader who cares to look."[15]

Werner Jeanrond in his *Theological Hermeneutics* concludes: "'Antioch' and 'Alexandria' then stand for two different hermeneutical paradigms: 'Antioch' studied the text's open message and assessed the text's spiritual quality in a literal manner, whereas 'Alexandria' disclosed the text's spiritual sense from the perspective of an overall theological knowledge."[16] With Jeanrond we might feel inclined to argue that Antioch, with its literal-grammatical method, is more open, whereas Alexandria is guided by a distinct doctrinal profile. Antiochenes are generally more open to new theological discoveries, whereas Alexandrians tend to defend a certain theological status quo. Jeanrond suggests that these two positions mark the two poles between which Christian hermeneutics was to develop further during the centuries to come. He points out that "[i]n a sense, all forms of theological hermeneutics are variations of these two poles."[17] An interpreter either respects the texts on their own terms, or reads them through the lens of a particular tradition.[18] Examples of the Alexandrian type may be found in various kinds of orthodoxies: whether guided by church authorities, such as the Council of Trent in reaction to the hermeneutics of the Reformation; or, informed by a radical emphasis on revelation, such as the theology of Karl Barth; or, in fundamentalisms, guided by verbal inspiration theories. Friedrich Schleiermacher's call for a philosophical theory of understanding and Rudolf Bultmann's project of demythologization each represent the Antiochene type of project.

In practice, it might not be possible to identify every hermeneutical position as a reflection of either Antioch or Alexandria, of either Aristotle or Plato. Such an either-or is not even desirable. One might prefer to have Aristotle on the table and still have Plato in the room. Indeed, Augustine already combines and transcends this polarity. He advocates a semiotic framework, an Antiochene trait, and an overarching guiding principle, a rule of faith defining spiritual praxis, which is an Alexandrian dimension.[19] In that sense, Augustine—and many interpreters with him—propagates a synthesis of letter and spirit.

Hermeneutics in the 20th century

Overlooking fifteen centuries of history, I make a giant leap to some milestones in 20th century hermeneutics. Hans-Georg Gadamer's (1900-2002) work *Truth and Method* was a major achievement.[20] With Heidegger, he affirms the significance of language as more than just a medium of communication. He distances himself from Dilthey's separation of *understanding* as the key concept of the humanities from *explanation* as the key concept in the natural sciences. Gadamer holds that hermeneutics is not merely the methodological basis for the humanities. Rather, it is at the root of every adequate understanding of all phenomena. Hence, it matters for the natural sciences as much as for the humanities. It is a practical philosophy. According to Gadamer, the fusion of the horizons of the text and of the reader is what brings about understanding.[21] The term *horizon* captures the insight that both the text (not necessarily literally understood as written words) and the interpreter are positioned in and conditioned by time, place and a number of circumstances. Gadamer argues that a fusion of horizons is achieved by a constant back and forth between our world and the world of the text. From an initial pre-understanding the reader addresses questions to the text; the text in turn affects the reader's own understanding. The reader asks additional questions and so on. Through this dynamic process the text reshapes the reader's self-understanding. Ideally, the horizons become fused. What is often called the hermeneutical circle is rather a spiraling forth. In any case, it means understanding by participation. This ideal process—the fusion of horizons—may in reality not be as happy and harmonious as the term suggests. Critics have accused Gadamer of being overly optimistic on this point. Philosophically speaking, the process of understanding and communication is always in danger of ideological distortion. Theologically speaking, the hermeneutical process is also subject to the brokenness inherent in post-lapsarian creation. Nevertheless, Gadamer's work reveals the historical situatedness of both the text and the reader, as well as the critical role of pre-understanding in the hermeneutical process.

Where Gadamer took a rather anti-methodological stance, Paul Ricoeur argues for the application of a multiplicity of methods without buying into their ideological superstructure. The aim is not to get access to a sense and meaning *behind* the text, that is, to understand the author better than he or she understood himself or herself. Rather, the aim is to grasp the meaning *in front of* it. Understanding is not about reconstructing the original intentions behind the text, but about what points towards a possible world, about its reference to new worlds or new "modes-of-being-in-the-world."[22]

By this development, the notion of *otherness* entered the discourse of interpretation. When otherness is taken seriously, it encourages a plurality of readings and acknowledges the otherness within the interpreter. Neo-orthodox models of interpretation tend to allocate otherness to God only and restrict themselves to an ad hoc use of philosophical models as ancillary concepts; I call this exclusive otherness. More radical hermeneutical models try to acknowledge otherness everywhere; I call this inclusive otherness. Hence, these latter models cannot do without true interdisciplinarity, that is, a mutually critical relation between theology and other sciences.

In this sense, our hermeneutics directly influences the agenda of the science-religion dialogue (or rather, it should more than it does). In the case of exclusive otherness, a theological agenda or an a priori (scientific) truth claim is key to the expected dialogue. The second model proceeds according to an agenda of *semper reformanda* (always in need of reformation): an unfinished search for truth, always open to new scrutiny and revision. All interpretations are considered to be approximate at best. My sympathies lie with the second model. Or, maybe more accurately, I try to stretch toward the second model as much as possible without losing touch with the ground.

Hermeneutics in religion-and-science

In 2002, a religion-and-science conference stated that hermeneutics matters, both in science and in religion.[23] It also found that issues of hermeneutics probably have played less of a role for the religion-and-science dialogue than they should have. Does this add something radically new to the dialogue? Some might argue that the hermeneutical question is not as new to the dialogue as I make it sound. Hasn't it been present in discussions about the philosophy of science and the philosophy of the dialogue itself? For example, the question whether critical realism or naturalism provides an adequate epistemological framework or not for the religion-and-science dialogue, is a hermeneutical question. Yet, it is my opinion that hermeneutics in religion and science in the future needs to reach beyond the search for an adequate epistemological framework. Good theology is always more, but never less than hermeneutics. Likewise, a good dialogue between religion and science should always be more, but never less than hermeneutics. In order to make the case for that statement, I will first take a look at the role of language.

Thinkers of the Enlightenment such as Immanuel Kant were, in principle, content with time and space as the a priori categories of the mind. They neglected, however, the integration of the category of language. The concept of language is crucial in hermeneutics. On a very elementary and experiential level, everybody who works and lives in and with more than one language knows that a language is more than just an ephemeral phenomenon. Transferring a thought from one language to another is more than just changing a dress. With language comes conceptualities, structures and allusions to traditions and cultures. This applies especially to the language of love and of prayer—it usually takes a while to find expressions for both love and prayer in a new language.

It may be less widely known and still less accepted that this contingency of language applies also to rational and scientific reasoning. Yet, there are scientists who have realized the problem. It is one of the important but often overlooked merits of some of the fathers of quantum physics to have observed and discussed the role of language. Both Niels Bohr and Werner Heisenberg spent time and effort reflecting on the role of language in general and in the natural sciences in particular. They rightly noticed that language is not an individual but an interpersonal skill. It is learned only in interaction. "Language is," reports Heisenberg, from a conversation with Bohr, "as it were, a net spread out between people, a net in which our thoughts and knowledge are inextricably enmeshed."[24] In spite of what they call the "strange, fluid character" of language, both seem to agree that the language of mathematical formulae at some point has to pass over into everyday language.[25] "For if we want to say anything at all about nature—and what else does science try to do?—we must somehow pass from mathematical to everyday language."[26] Bohr and Heisenberg conducted these conversations with a couple of colleagues and friends around Easter 1933 in a rather basic Alpine skiing hut. Bent over the washbasin one night, Bohr clothes his new insights with an earthy metaphor:

> Our washing up is just like our language... We have dirty water and dirty dishcloths, and yet we manage to get the plates and glasses clean. In language, too, we have to work with unclear concepts and a form of logic whose scope is restricted in an unknown way, and yet we use it to bring some clarity in our understanding of nature.[27]

With Bohr, we must acknowledge that language is marked by an abundance of ambiguity, with myriads possibilities of combining word-elements. The sentences we build do not resemble neat brick walls. Rather, they look like the fickle waves in Bohr's washbasin. Indeed, this seems to be the way it needs to be: ambiguity renders the diversity needed for evolution; univocality would put an end to development.

From these conversations, Heisenberg emerges as a hopeful bridge builder between idealism and realism, trying to find possibilities beyond the limits of Aristotelian logic.[28] He experiments with different levels of logic: non-Aristotelian forms would be valid on intermediate levels, while Aristotelian logic would remain valid on the highest level. Bohr appears as an optimistic pragmatist: language is terribly imprecise, yet it works. Einstein remains in this respect more of a pessimistic idealist, concerned as he is with a Lord who is "raffiniert, aber nicht boshaft," subtle but not malicious.[29]

The Alpine ski hut setting is worth a hermeneutical comment. In his book *Beyond Physics*, Heisenberg describes an atmosphere reminiscent of a Platonic symposium: a number of top scientists taking an Easter vacation in the Alps, skiing and talking, meeting in the mountains during summer time, walking and talking – playing around with thoughts and ideas about physics, about philosophy, about music, about culture, and sometimes doing nothing. As far as I recall, Heisenberg never mentions any grant proposals they had to write or any foundations that would not accept their projects. Of course, this all happened years before the tragic reality occurred that Michael Frayn has described in his play *Copenhagen*, so there is no reason to romanticize the life and work of the scientific community before World War II. Yet, ideas on which conditions facilitate intellectual creativity are worth thinking about.

Reflection on language and interpretation has often focused on the hermeneutical process of the *individual*.[30] In addition, we need to ask how interpretations relate to judgments of a whole community of scholar on what is and what is not an adequate description of reality. The development of language, be it scientific or theological, is a social and communal process. Moving from the awareness of the role of language to a full-fledged hermeneutical discourse requires extensive work. A detailed description of the geography of that journey would go beyond the limits of this talk. Therefore, I will restrict myself to just seven remarks.

1. A hermeneutical approach sharpens our sensibility to how the *interplay of religious, philosophical and scientific views* has shaped not only the interpretation and understanding of science and scientific results, but also the motivation for engaging in scientific activity at all. Here I will focus on interpretations rather than motivations. After all, motivations can be mistaken and still render good results. Friedrich Nietzsche (1844-1900), who during his lifetime witnessed significant developments in science, has somewhat sarcastically pointed out that science has been promoted mainly because of three errors:

> [P]artly because it was through science that one hoped best to understand God's goodness and wisdom—the main motive in the soul of the great Englishmen (such as Newton); partly because one believed in the absolute usefulness of knowledge, especially in the most intimate affiliation between morality, knowledge, and happiness—the main motive in the soul of the

> French (such as Voltaire); and partly because one believed that in science one had and loved something selfless, harmless, self-sufficient, and truly innocent in which the evil drives of humanity had no part at all—the main motive in the soul of Spinoza, who felt divine in attaining knowledge—in sum, because of three errors.[31]

Nietzsche declares the motives wrong. Yet, he does not call into question the success of scientific inquiry.

Having said this, I will leave the question of motivation as such aside and turn to the question of interpretation, which, of course, in some ways remains linked to the issue of motivations. A scientist once claimed that Heisenberg and Bohr were able to come up with uncertainty and complementarity because they were familiar with thinking in terms of mystery and paradox because of their immersion in crucial features of their religion.[32] I do not support this particular claim. Still, I do think that there is evidence enough to state that scientific language has been shaped in interaction with religious and philosophical language, sometimes in beneficial, sometimes in misleading ways. Let me tell you a story that I think is better suited to prove my point. This story could be entitled, *Newton contra Leibniz: A Story About the Lack of Hermeneutics.*

It is well-known that Newton and Leibniz did not like each other very well. One of the reasons why they could not agree is revealed in the correspondence between Leibniz and Newton's friend and disciple Samuel Clarke.[33] From November 1715 to Leibniz' death in 1716, the two debated a couple of issues. They focused especially on whether time and space are absolute or relative. Newton and Clarke held the absoluteness of both, whereas Leibniz argued for their relativity.

It is interesting to note that Leibniz and Clarke's disagreement concerning space and time is paralleled by a difference in their understanding of what is the first and foremost of God's attributes.

For Newton and Clarke, the clarity of absoluteness and determinism calls for a God who is one—Newton detested the doctrine of the Trinity[34]—and whose foremost attribute is power, understood as omnipotence and omnipresence. For the inventor of the calculus (especially in Newton's form as opposed to Leibniz's), it makes perfect sense to conceptualize God above all as the determiner of the initial conditions. Only well defined starting conditions guarantee a well-defined solution of a differential equation. God's omnipotence and the elegance of the calculus make a perfect couple.[35]

Clarke follows Newton in clinging to omnipotence and omnipresence. Leibniz, however, offers *wisdom* as God's most prominent quality. As far as I can see from their correspondence, neither of them reflected on the nature and process of the interpretations they were making all the time. Theological interpretations informed their scientific statements, and scientific models informed their theological positions.

More hermeneutics would certainly have been helpful. In other words, if these great thinkers had spent as much energy on the art of suspicion (in the sense I am using it here) as they spent on the art of being mad at each other, the Newton/Clarke-Leibniz controversy might have looked very different. In this case there was simply too little awareness of how interpretation matters.

Another famous example of the mutual influence of scientific and religious concepts can be found in the thought of Albert Einstein. In his case, it is well known how clearly his problems with a dice-throwing God resonate with his repugnance to some of the implications of quantum theory.[36] Einstein would have been far better off if he had reflected on the image of God he was presupposing and whether contemporary theologians presupposed the same image when they speak of God.

Einstein is not the only scientist who clung to theological concepts that most contemporary theologians had abandoned. It has been shown that more recent cosmological theories still follow the same theological pattern as Einstein had in his mind. In an article from 1995, James F. Moore has analyzed newer cosmological concepts that physicists use when they present their cosmology in connection with theological statements. Having examined texts by Frank Tipler, Stephen Hawking, Paul Davies and Steven Weinberg, Moore comes to the following conclusion: "God is again identified with the abstract mathematical structure that governs the evolutionary process of the universe. God, basically reduced to the total interaction of all forces in a comprehensible and comprehensive theory, is again identified with the one in control."[37]

Many of us, perhaps even the majority of us, who participate in the dialogue between religion and science are obliged to use writings that scientists themselves have popularized, probably not in our own discipline, but often in all those disciplines that are not covered by our expertise. From a hermeneutical point of view it is worth noting that many of these books present a combination of what might be called "thick science and thin theology" or "new science and old theology."

2. The critical discussion of Thomas Kuhn's *concept of paradigm* and its role in so-called scientific revolutions has rendered some precious hermeneutical insights. If the Newton-Leibniz controversy can be entitled *About the Lack of Hermeneutics*, the debate that followed Kuhn's *The Structure of Scientific Revolutions* may be labeled *Nothing but Hermeneutics?*

Thomas Kuhn launched his famous theory of paradigm shifts in 1962.[38] In his well-known thesis that paradigms structure observation and define reality, Kuhn applies an historical and sociological perspective: pre-paradigmatic periods in science are followed by a time when a valid paradigm allows, what Kuhn calls, "normal science" to take place. Under the conditions of normal science and its "strong network of commitments—conceptual, theoretical, instrumental and methodological,"[39] the community of researchers concentrates on the routine activity of "puzzle-solving" without testing the paradigm itself. However, in due time, an increasing number of observed anomalies leads to a crisis and eventually to a revolution and to the establishment of a new paradigm that is incommensurable with the old one. A paradigm shift has traits of conversion and revolution.

The Kuhnian concept was meant to provide a hermeneutical model of understanding development and change in the natural sciences. Criticisms targeted the vagueness of his concept of *paradigm* both in definition and in use, his idea of the *incommensurability* of the old and the new paradigm, and the notion of *revolution* as a description of development in science. Kuhn was charged with subjectivity, irrationality and relativism. The change of paradigm, which Kuhn described as "the selection by conflict within the scientific community of the fittest way to practice future science" resulting in "an increase in articulation and specialization,"[40] was said to belong to the realm of the social psychology of discovery rather than to the philosophy of science, because the change follows values rather than formal rules. What makes the Kuhn case so interesting, apart from the mentioned criticisms, is the fact that his hermeneutical concept initiated a process of criticism of the hermeneutical concept and process itself, which turned out to be fruitful in various respects. Both in its initial and its modified shape Kuhn's concept of paradigm has contributed to a number of achievements.

First, it highlighted the historical situatedness of scientific research and the role of consensus in rationality. Research does not happen in a historical, political and cultural vacuum. Although successful researchers can be idiosyncratic loners, in the end their theories will not make it without the support of the scientific community. Second, the concept of paradigm lifted up the interplay of scientific and non-scientific components in the development of science. For instance, it shed light upon the ambiguity of commitment as that which can both undercut rationality and make scientific work successful. On the one hand, commitment can create biases that make blind; on the other hand commitment can appear as the source of energy that achieves the seemingly impossible. Third, Kuhn's concept acknowledged the circularity of abstracting data into a paradigm (or theory) that informs the selection and interpretation of new data. Thus it contributed to fostering an interest in the sociology of scientific knowledge and in the hermeneutics of holistic non-universalist rationality.

Although the concept of paradigm has been followed by alternative concepts such as competing research programs (Imre Lakatos) and research traditions (Larry Laudan), it has had an impact on the relation between science and religion. Among the enduring fruits of the post-Kuhnian debate I would count: a broadened concept of rationality and an affirmation of the complexity and contextuality of rationality; a constructive discussion on the translatability of various discourses; a critique that questions the self-assuring power of paradigms, calling for an examination of the roles not only of culture in general, huge though that influence is, but also of race, gender, age, and political and economic power in the process of forming guiding ideas; and, an exploration of discourses that call themselves postfoundationalist.[41]

From what I have said so far, one could easily get the impression that the impact of the post-Kuhnian debate was predominantly negative, in the sense that it seemed to be more about tearing down than building up: biases were dismantled and objectivity was called into question. The first naïveté of trust in simple and objective truth is lost forever. Yet, a focus on interpretation and hermeneutics does not rule out the focus on rationality. The quest for truth is as viable as ever, but it has become more complicated or even more complex. Therefore, I would like to mention yet another positive by-product of the post-Kuhnian debate, namely the positive appreciation of non-linear and non-intentional processes and their significance for progress in science. In a positivist culture, scientific discoveries that happen by chance are almost an embarrassment. At least they are supposed to happen only as rare exceptions that confirm the rule that scientific activity is based on intentionality, on experiments and rational conclusions. In a post-Kuhnian world it is much easier to acknowledge the role of coincidence and chance in the development of science. It becomes legitimate to take into consideration the role of this remarkable combination of chance, attention and power of combination called serendipity.[42] Obviously, serendipity plays a part also in the birth of scientific and technological innovation. Among the most famous examples we find Alexander Fleming's 1928 discovery of the mould that led to the development of penicillin. Wilhelm Conrad Röntgen's discovery of the X-ray in 1895 would be another one.

3. Hermeneutical reflection has taught us *suspicion toward singular forms* ("singular" in the grammatical, not the mathematical sense). We have realized the need to acknowledge the diversity of the different bodies of knowledge. Rather than science per se, we speak of sciences. Rather than of religion or theology, we speak of religions and theologies. The study of the sciences in terms of history, sociology, pedagogy and psychology of sciences also adds new hermeneutical dimensions to the scientific discourse. In a similar way, the study of religion in terms of history, sociology, pedagogy and psychology of religions adds extra dimensions not only to the understanding of religions themselves but to the religion-and-science dialogue—making it ever more obvious that scientists of different disciplines and theologians from different traditions need each other.

4. Hermeneutical analysis has also shed light on the process of how models, metaphors or theories that are successful in one area extend their influence to a whole range of different areas. Scientific vocabulary has what I call a potential for building *ideology*, which should not be underestimated. Scientific concepts influence areas outside their original homeland. They are also subject to reverse influence from other areas. For example, the successful use of the one force of gravitation to explain the mechanics of both heaven and earth triggered an enthusiastic search for the one principle and unified structure in many other areas.[43] The concept of evolution has set off, and still does, more or less imaginative accounts of development in various areas of knowledge. The formulation of the principle of complementarity prompted explanations in terms of complementary relationships outside of its original context. Simplicity, complexity and beauty are other keywords that live a complicated life inside and outside of both religion and science. The exploration of the significance of this life has only just begun.[44] Hermeneutics is a necessary tool to access and to assess these processes of migration of what Isabelle Stengers has called "concepts nomades."[45]

5. It goes without saying that hermeneutical investigations need to be conducted in an interdisciplinary mode. *Interdisciplinarity* means mutual acknowledgement of different disciplines as distinct and complicated bodies of knowledge. In religion-and-science circles this may sound self-evident, but it really isn't. There is still a popular misunderstanding that science is the field for experts whereas religion is a field for everybody. You need to show your expertise in order to talk astrophysics or molecular biology, but you need not have any particular training to talk religion and theology (the latter understood as the critical and self-critical reflection about the content and effects of religious traditions). That way, we have often ended up with what I just called a mixture of thick science and thin theology or new science and outdated theology.

6. Another misconception to challenge is the assumption that the sciences are always in *progress* while theology stands still and always looks back. We know it is not true. It happens that scientists look back and often pick up theories and models from the past, revisiting what seemed to be blind alleys in the history of science. For example, Christiaan Huygens's wave theory of light, published in 1678, came to be overshadowed by a particle theory. In Newton's physics, photons proved to be the adequate understanding of the nature of light. The formulation of the principle of complementarity in the 20th century encouraged scientists to revisit Huygens and his principle.

The fact that theology is changing all the time is not hard to prove. Theology is not the same after the probing of process thought, existentialist philosophy, and the development of various liberation theologies, to mention just a few 20th century examples. Christology is not the same after the different quests for the historical Jesus. Theological thought is not the same after the renaissance of Trinitarian theology since the 1980s. Theology has certainly changed radically by becoming more interdisciplinary. Yet, scientists and philosophers sometimes behave as if there were no difference between theologies at the time of Galileo, Newton, Darwin, Einstein or Hawking.

7. Finally, hermeneutics itself faces the seemingly impossible task of providing a *critique of the hermeneutical process itself*. Hermeneutics helps us understand the contextuality of science, but that does not mean that hermeneutic methods are themselves beyond context. The very tools we use to detect and understand biases and ideologies are very likely to be charged with biases themselves. Here context matters. The process behind and around research matters too, not only the results. The consequences, which might arise far from the origin, likewise also matter. This applies to the detonation of a bomb far from its scientific origins, as well as to less tragic and spectacular processes. If, for example, Bruno Latour is right in his essay, *Give Me a Laboratory and I Will Raise the World*, then we should pay more attention to laboratories as spaces "where the future reservoirs of political power are in the making" and to the costs of the construction and transformation of society according to laboratory experiments.[46] This also implies that we need to take a critical look at what "the market" means to science as well as to religion. The market has developed into an anonymous power, at times acting irrationally, irrespective of national borders, exercising enormous influence by moving index figures a fraction of a percent up or down.

For a long time it seemed that the impact of economics wasn't a proper theme for a decent dialogue between science and religion. To some it sounds like too crude a question, for others a question too complicated to address, and too far away from pure science and pure theology. However, it is ridiculously obvious that science and religion are also subject to the economic structures governing the societies in which these activities are pursued. The increase of privately funded research in biotechnology over against publicly funded academic projects impacts the agenda. It certainly matters who funds research activities and education and who pays for the results. It certainly matters globally whose questions are allowed to be on the top of the agenda and whose interests never make it to the table. It certainly matters throughout the world who benefits from something in the first place, who in the second and third place, and who will probably never do so.[47] We need to be able to place our own areas of knowledge on a global map. Cyberspace often creates the illusion that space does not matter. It does.

These are all examples of issues that point to the importance of hermeneutical reflection. Most certainly, this reflection will not lift us up to a position of serene clarity. Rather it will force us into what theologian Rita Nakashima Brock has called "life in the messy middle of things."[48] The messy middle of things is not the most glorious place we can think of, but for the sake of credibility, I think the dialogue between religion and science needs to be taken there, and needs to take place there. If the dialogue is not helpful in the messy middle of life, we should spend our lifetime on other things.

The Challenge from Feminisms

In this lecture, I will give some examples of how *feminist research* analyzes the consequences of the interplay of masculine, feminine and gender typologies in religion and science. Sketches from the history of science as well as current scientific conceptualizations indicate that beliefs in the inferiority of women form part of our inherited scientific, religious and metaphysical framework. Drawing from hermeneutics, feminist scholarship and complexity theory, in the last part of the lecture, I will outline some new ways of approaching the theological locus, "God and creation."

Feminine Imagery in the History of Science

At the age of forty-one or forty-two, probably in 1602 or 1603, the great Francis Bacon ponders the right method for transmitting scientific knowledge.[1] Looking for the right interpretation and the right pedagogy, he writes a monologue addressed to a young man whom he calls "son." It is what we know as the fragment, *The Masculine Birth of Time*. Bacon offers blistering criticisms of many of the great thinkers—he calls them "the whole mob of professorial teachers"—and asks whether or not someone will "recite the formula by which I may devote them all to oblivion."[2] Aristotle "composed an art or manual of madness and made us slaves of words."[3] "Your philosophy, Plato, was but scraps of borrowed information polished and strung together. ... you took men's minds off their guard ... you turned our minds away from observation ... you taught us to turn our mind's eye inward and grovel before our own blind and confused idols under the name of contemplative philosophy."[4] On Paracelsus: "You have a passion for taking your idols in pairs and dreaming up mutual imitations, correspondences, parallelisms, between the products or your elements."⁵ "By mixing the divine with the natural, the profane with the sacred, heresies with mythology, you have corrupted ... both human and religious truth."⁶ Hence, Bacon concludes, "it would not be a proper thing for me, who am preparing things useful for the future of the human race, to bury myself in the study of ancient literature."⁷ Because, "... generally speaking science is to be sought from the light of nature, not from the darkness of antiquity. It matters not what has been done; our business is to see what can be done."⁸

This forms the background of his own agenda, an agenda that has been influential far beyond his own lifetime:

> My intention is to impart to you, not the figments of my own brain, nor the shadows thrown by words, nor a mixture of religion and science, nor a few commonplace observations or notorious experiments tricked out to make a composition as fanciful as a stage-play. No; I am come in very truth leading to you Nature with all her children to bind her to your service and make her your slave. ... So may it go with me, my son; so may I succeed in my only earthly wish, namely to stretch the deplorably narrow limits of man's dominion over the universe to their promised bounds; ... ⁹

> My dear, dear boy, what I purpose is to unite you with *things themselves* in a chaste, holy, and legal wedlock; and from this association you will secure an increase beyond all the hopes and prayers of ordinary marriages, to wit, a blessed race of Heroes or Supermen who will overcome the immeasurable helplessness and poverty of the human race, ... Take heart, then, my son, and give yourself to me so that I may restore you to yourself.¹⁰

What we see here is an intricate play with male and female typology. It comes in two flavors, so to speak. On the one hand we have nature with all her children to be bound to service and slavery. In the Preface of Bacon's *Novum Organum*, sexual imagery is very obvious: When "a true son of science ... has left the antechambers of nature trodden by the multitude, an entrance at last may be discovered to her inner apartments."[11] Here, "the secrets of nature betray themselves more readily when tormented by art,"[12] as Bacon says later in the same book. This sounds like what has been described as the spirit of the English Royal Society: the male scientist subdues female nature, penetrates her and forces her to reveal her secrets.[13] Or, more poetically expressed in Thomas Sprat's History of the Royal Society: "The Beautiful Bosom of *Nature* will be Expos'd to our view: we shall enter into its *Garden*, and tast [sic] of its *Fruits*, and satisfy our selves with its *plenty*."[14]

This represents one side of female imagery: wild nature that needs to be subdued. The contrasting image is science, the virgin. Bacon talks about the scientist's holy and chaste wedlock to science. In Bacon's world, science is also female, and powerfully so: "... science must be such as to select her followers, who must be worthy to be adopted into her family."[15] Science is the saint who gathers her followers in monastery-like noble communities, whereas nature is the wild woman that needs to be forced into submission. Variations of this typology have survived well into modern times. The presentation of woman as either virgin or whore has been observed in many areas, not least in religion. It may still come as a surprise that it has also influenced the understanding and self-understanding of science and scientists.

Let me give you just one example: In his 1965 Nobel Lecture, Richard Feynman did what he called "something of less value," namely describing not only the facts but also the process behind his work on quantum electrodynamics. This, he says, is of value neither scientifically, nor for understanding the development of ideas; its only value is "to make the lecture more entertaining"[16] — a viewpoint surprisingly unaware of the hermeneutical perspectives

I raised in my previous lecture. Toward the end of his lecture, Feynman concludes:

> So what happened to the old theory that I fell in love with as a youth? Well, I would say it's become an old lady, that has very little attractive left in her ... But, we can say the best we can for any old woman, that she has been a very good mother and she has given birth to some very good children.[17]

This may sound playful and can be taken as an unfortunate but insignificant attempt to make a lecture more enjoyable, in other words, a mere trifle. Yet, I think that trifles often have a revelatory character. They help detect distortions of truth about facts. Critique of what appears to be adiaphorous often opens the door for a much more thorough and significant critique.

Feminism has offered many examples of such critique and developed a solid record of scholarship. The time when some people could think that feminism is just the playground for a few wild women is definitely gone. It is no longer only women who explore and apply feminist perspectives. In this talk, I will not focus on feminist theory in general. Nor do I focus very much on feminist critique of theology, even though I think such a critique is relevant and necessary. Yet, my emphasis today is predominantly on a feminist critique of science, especially the use of religiously motivated feminine stereotypes.

In this respect, feminist scholars have developed this critique in three main areas:
a) They have raised issues of ethics and politics that are basically *human issues*, equally involving women, men, children and the nature we all relate to;
b) They have addressed issues of *exclusion and inclusion* of women and their work, and of minorities and their cultures, especially focusing on the use of religious themes in science;
c) They have demonstrated how gender categories are

informing and biasing both research agendas and the interpretation of data, while analyzing and suggesting *different ways of doing science*.

There is today ample evidence of the relevance and success of feminist scholarship in the first two areas. The third area is much more difficult, but certainly not less interesting and important. While it is still relatively easy to argue that biases influence the interpretation of data and the questions that lead to a research agenda, it is much more difficult to argue whether or in what sense feminist critique would actually lead to "a different kind of science." But let us first turn to the first two areas, namely common human issues and matters of exclusion and inclusion.

Feminist Critique of Science

A number of scholars have provided analyses of gender relations, arising from biological, social and cultural conditions, which are a matter for both sexes, and not just for feminists. Only a few can be mentioned here.

Carolyn Merchant[18] has described how during the 16th and 17th centuries the image of an organic cosmos with a living female earth at its center was replaced by a mechanistic world view in which nature was reconstructed as dead and passive, to be dominated and controlled by humans. She uses the history of mining as an example of how feminine imagery of nature was used. The ecofeminist perspective that emerges from Merchant's analysis is somehow reflective of much of women's interdisciplinary scholarship in science and religion. Indian ecologist and activist Vandana Shiva would be another example of this kind of scholarship.[19]

Londa Schiebinger[20] has described many nuances of the

dynamics of gender in the history of science, such as the interplay of representations of science in female and male symbols. She has given numerous examples of the manifold contributions of women in the realm of the sciences as well as of the obstacles they met. And she has argued that with the disappearance of female symbolism in the scientific culture in the late 18th century, the history of science was rewritten in a way that diminished or excluded the achievements made by women.

As these short remarks show, feminine imagery is not "good" or "bad" in itself. It has to be understood in context with the connotations and associations that surround it. For example, feminine nature in the Baconian sense entices men into subduing and exploiting nature, whereas earth understood as mother Gaia tends to evoke an attitude of reverence and ecological consciousness,

Mary Midgley[21] has repeatedly explored the religious dimensions of science. Also, John Barrow has pointed to religiously motivated enthusiasm as the root for the powerful concept of laws of nature:

> Our monotheistic traditions reinforce the assumption that the Universe is at root a unity, that it is not governed by different legislation in different places ... Our Western religious tradition also endows us with the assumption that things are governed by a logic that exists independently of those things, that laws are externally imposed as though they were the decrees of a transcendent divine legislator.[22]

I do not know whether Stephen Hawking made the connection between a Theory of Everything and knowing the mind of God out of conviction or in order to make the book a best-seller, but both the retail success of *A Brief History of Time* and the long history of this kind of connection suggest that there is something important going on here. Margaret Wertheim[23] has pointed out that from

Pythagoras to Kepler, Newton, Boskovitch, Faraday, Einstein and beyond, scientific research has been fueled by a religious belief in the unity and harmony of nature—with mathematical man as the high priest of science.

Where Barrow stops with the analysis of the mutual reinforcement of the concept of monotheism and the concept of laws of nature and where Hawking sticks to the intimation of God getting into trouble if we start knowing too much, Wertheim takes a few more steps. She claims that the combination of God and laws of nature releases a normative power, resulting in the moral obligation to look for grand unified theories and the Theory of Everything. Following this obligation is not without consequences. A "Yes" to the resources this takes is a "No" to other kinds of research. She asks critically: For whom is this? On what grounds are enormous mental and material resources invested into the race for a Theory of Everything? What is defensible from a social justice point of view and what is not? Her thesis that physics is like the Catholic Church of science, which to the very last denies women priesthood, may seem a bit overdone. On the other hand, reflecting on the presence of women in the dialogue between religion and science seems to suggest that there might be the possibility that Wertheim has a point here. In 2002, the International Society for Science and Religion (ISSR) was founded in Granada, Spain. Membership is by election only. At the founding meeting of this society, membership consisted of 90 men and 8 women. As of Spring 2003, its executive council consisted of 10 males. David Noble[24] has made points similar to Wertheim's about the religious roots of science and technological enchantment.

The parallels between science and ecclesiastical authoritarianism have not only been critiqued from a feminist viewpoint. From a Native American perspective, Vine Deloria, Jr. has come to comparable conclusions. European thinkers have failed, argues Deloria, because "[s]cience and philosophy simply copied the institutional paths already taken by Western religion and mystified themselves.... Institutionalization of science ... meant that scientists would come to act like priests ...,"[25] and he adds, "[a]s many lies are told to protect scientific doctrine as were ever told to protect 'the church.'"[26] True or not, the effects on American Indians Deloria points to, resemble very much what feminist writers have observed concerning the position of women. They have often been used as objects of research, as informants, but have not been regarded as fellow-researchers and partners. Deloria's work alerts us to the fact that gender constructions are not the only ones that can be detrimental. An exclusive focus on the polarization in male and female gender is almost as dangerous as a concentration on the male as the representation of the 'true truth.' Factors like race, class, age, culture and ethnicity are part of the picture, too. Barbara Ann Holmes's book *Race and the Cosmos: An Invitation to View the World Differently*[27] illustrates, from an African-American perspective, the need of expanding feminist perspectives beyond the point where we work with abstract universalized constructions of male and female.

In her book *The Less Noble Sex*, Nancy Tuana has demonstrated the reflective and constructive impact of scientific, philosophical and religious conceptions of woman. Surveying thought on the subject from Hesiod's *Theogony* to Freud's psychology, she concludes, "belief in woman's inherent inferiority ... remains a part of the fabric of Western culture."[28] The belief that women are less perfect, less evolved, less divine, less rational, less moral, less healthy than men, and hence are in need of control, forms part of our inherited metaphysics.[29] This belief nurtures the construction of maleness and femaleness in relation to the subject matters of science as well as in relation to the role of the scientist, as Sharon Traweek has pointed out in her essay *Pilgrim's Progress: Male Tales*

Told during a Life in Physics. She argues that models of success and failure in a community of scholars—in this case, the physics lab—are not gender-free, neither in form nor in content. The way success is defined shows some striking similarities to the social construction of male gender in Western culture. Feynman is not the only physicist who talks about nature or his ideas about nature in terms of "a singular female love object," an object to love, unveil, and know.[30] The social construction of gender underlying this imagery is that female human beings are more passive and less aggressive than man. This difference is then used as a definition of the relation between scientists and their love objects. Traweek's description echoes what we have come to recognize as the Baconian mind-set: "The scientist is persistent, dominant, and aggressive, ultimately penetrating the corpus of secrets mysteriously concealed by a passive, albeit elusive nature."[31]

It is certainly illuminating to undertake a study of how these typologies actually influence the way science is conceptualized. However, feminist discourse has discussed more than that. From the exploration of how gender is constructed and the study of how categories of sex are applied in religion and science, feminist research has moved on to an analysis of how these constructions operate in various areas of scientific theory and praxis. In this sense, the focus is on different ways of doing science—what I described as the third area of feminist research of special relevance for religion-and-science. The question is, does feminism lead to different ways of doing science? Does it lead to a different science? The answer seems to be no, if we think of the abstractness and universality of the laws of nature. It seems absurd to think that laws of nature are gender sensitive. The more abstract the science the more difficult it is to argue for the significance of a gender perspective. At least, I think it would be difficult to show the relevance of gender perspective in particle physics. It appears to be much easier in sciences like anthropology. But let us look at some examples that lie in between theoretical physics and anthropology.

Nancy Howell and others have argued that interpretations of the interaction between sperm and egg and the cell nucleus and cytoplasm in terms of marriage metaphors have been misleading.[32] In the 1930s, Howell tells us, four competing theories, all based on the marriage metaphor, were used to describe the relationship of nucleus and cytoplasm. The passage is worth quoting at length:

> One German model described the cell like an autocratic Prussian family with the nucleus as the executive decision maker and the cytoplasm as obedient to its commands. American geneticist, T. H. Morgan, used the American family, in particular his marriage, as a metaphor which implied that nucleus and cytoplasm confer as husband and wife do and then the nucleus makes the final decision about what the cytoplasm will do. British socialist, C. H. Waddington, used his marriage as metaphor and described the relationship of nucleus and cell as a partnership of equals. E. E. Just, Black American embryologist, proposed that the nucleus dominated the cytoplasm, which passively responded to the vitality of the nucleus.[33]

Howell states that "[A]lthough contemporary biologists are aware that nucleus and cytoplasm are interactive, the power of the metaphor continues to influence portrayals of the nucleus as the controller of the cell processes."[34]

Examples like these reflect a deeply rooted structure of thought about knowledge, science, and the subjects and the objects of science, where again male tends to be associated with active, rational, public and dominant and female with passive, irrational/emotional, private and subordinate.

Emily Martin has examined the central images in popular and

scientific literature on immunology. She found an overwhelming presence of war vocabulary, such as battlefield, invasion, Blitzkrieg, mines, bombs blasting through the invader's cell membrane, execution. The body is seen in the image of a national state that seeks to identify intruders and put them out of action. It is about distinguishing self from non-self and to eliminate the latter, the other, either by means of the so-called killer T cells, often described with male associations, or by means of the less aggressive phagocytes. These are described as evolutionarily more primitive and they are, not surprisingly, linked with female associations.[35] In her search for alternative images of the body, Martin turns to the Polish biologist Ludwik Fleck who would rather "speak of a complicated revolution within the complex life unit than of an invasion of it."[36] If, instead of focusing on war imagery, more attention were given to the relation between microorganisms and macrophages, we would be more likely to reason in terms of ecological interdependency. Emily Martin notes: "Instead of a life and death struggle, with terrorism within and war at the borders, we would have a symbiosis within a life unit that encompasses the body and its environment ..."[37]

In addition to occurring in the lab, constructions like these take place in the field, and perhaps more frequently. Comparing Japanese and American research on great apes, Frans de Waal[38] has shown how conscious and unconscious paradigms—for instance about individualism and social behavior—inform a research agenda and the interpretation of data. Long before Western researchers started to ask questions about social behavior among monkeys and great apes, Japanese scholars had successfully studied patterns of communal behavior. These studies did not gain much international appreciation as long as the West was attached to an individual-centered agenda, epitomized by the idea of the selfish gene. Anthropologist Sarah Blaffer Hrdy, also looking at research practices in primatology, has argued that early studies of social behavior were distorted by a number of biases (ideological, methodological and observational) that in many cases made researchers overlook active roles played by females. Studies of baboons show that "[n]ot only are male-female relationships much more reciprocal and complex than previously realized, but there is also much more involvement by males with infants."[39] Can such biases be avoided? If yes, how? In her reflection on these questions, Hrdy is critical of simple revisionist strategies that would just replace one set of biases with another one. Rather, she encourages what one might call a hermeneutics of permanent multidirectional critical reassessment of scientific theory and praxis. In other words, she calls for both an examination of the epistemological underpinnings of research and an analysis of the socio-cultural parameters that tend to sneak into research agendas.

In terms of epistemology, Karen Barad has suggested an alternative that is informed by her research in feminism as well as by her reading of Niels Bohr. Barad develops what she has called the concept of agential realism as an epistemological and ontological framework. Agential realism takes into account that the practices of the sciences are not only descriptive, but also productive. As Niels Bohr once expressed it: "We are both bystanders and participants in the great drama of existence."[40] Yet, scientific practices are not mere social constructions, but "constrained by particular material-discursive factors."[41] In Barad's view,

> [a]gential realism is a feminist intervention in debates between realists and social constructivists. It provides an understanding of the nature of scientific practices which recognizes that objectivity and agency are bound up with issues of responsibility and accountability. ... Agential realism is not about representations of an independent reality but about

real consequences, interventions, creative possibilities, and responsibilities of intra-acting within the world.[42]

This overview indicates that today we are in possession of numerous contributions that spell out the challenge from various forms of feminisms. Sandra Harding's *Whose Science? Whose Knowledge?*, Nancy Howell's *A Feminist Cosmology*, Lucy Tatman's *Knowledge That Matters*, Sallie Mc Fague's *The Body of God*; as well as Evelyn Fox Keller, Donna Haraway, Vandana Shiva, Ann Pederson and Lisa Stenmark all incorporate feminism, science, technology and religion in their work.

The challenge from feminisms has been a journey in questioning: Who is speaking for whom? Who is speaking from which position? Whose experience and whose knowledge is taken as standard? What does something mean in the perspective of community? This is more than just reversing a flawed agenda. The acknowledgement that adequate representation, interpretation and application is a process far more complicated than not only Francis Bacon and his followers thought, but even we ourselves tend to believe, has consequences yet to be seen.

Up to now I have spent my lecture time thinking about hermeneutics and feminist approaches. Especially in the case of feminism, I have mostly focused on science, and you might rightly ask, where is the critique of theology? Of course, theological self-critique is constantly called for, in the light of hermeneutics as well as in the light of femist, womanist, Mujerista and other approaches. And I can assure you that feminist critiques of theology have been massive in all disciplines. Biblical studies, church history, systematic theology, ethics or the practical theological disciplines are no longer the same after the critiques of feminist research. Has feminism so far changed more in religion than in the sciences? Is it easier to influence religion than science? Are some sciences more apt to change than others? These are all questions we might wish to work with in our discussion.

For now, I think it is time to conclude with an example of how I imagine that hermeneutical and feminist theology can inform theological work in the light of the science-and-religion dialogue. I will use these resources to briefly revisit a classical theological locus, "God and Creation."

Hermeneutical and Feminist Suspicion Cultivated:
Creation and Complexity

In traditional understanding God has often been conceived of as the one who establishes order. Even though there is no chaos monster in Genesis 1, the formless void mentioned in Genesis 1:2 might suggest something like a chaos, out of which God creates order by separating things from each other and by providing a structure that prevents those things from collapsing again into an unstructured chaotic mess. God replaces chaotic mess with order; that is what the priestly account (Gen. 1:1-2:4a) seems to suggest. This is an order of rules. The second creation story beginning in Genesis 2:4b does not start from a formless void. Here, God appears as the gardener who needs water and creates it. This narrative presents an order of growth rather than an order as a set of rules, that is, something dynamic rather than static.

What can we make of this if we both want to honor the difference in the two accounts and incorporate a religion-and-science perspective that is sensitive to challenges posed by hermeneutics and feminisms? I will outline my answer to this question in the shape of a few remarks.

First of all, I would like to have us look beyond the notions of design and order. Actually, there is kind of an anti-order movement in contemporary Christian theology which is supported by several sources, namely liberation theologies (and here I count feminist theologies as liberation theologies), the renaissance of Trinitarian theology since the 1980s and the dialogue with other sciences. Theologian Elizabeth Johnson, drawing on feminist analysis, has suggested that it was the fear of chaos that motivated obsession with order in God, and that this obsession with order supports hierarchical and oppressive structures.[43] Even if only half of this were right, it is still worth trying it the other way round, at least in terms of a compelling thought experiment: embrace chaos! It sounds creative. Yet, as a reality we might not prefer chaos, even though chaos theory has helped us understand how life processes work, and how the interplay of chance and determinism can give birth to ordered structures without violation of the second law of thermodynamics. But chaos is still chaos.

Recently, interesting attempts have been made to invoke the concept of complexity, asking the question: how can we move focus from a concept that elevates order as a prevailing hermeneutical principle to a hermeneutics of complexity in creation theology? What do we need to think of in such a process of interpretation?

1. We need to be aware of the fact that trying out a hermeneutics of complexity is probably at least in part motivated by the temptation to jump up on the epistemological train of our time. Seventy-five years ago, the name of this epistemological train would probably have been complementarity.[44] In our days, the theme that seems to be addressed almost everywhere is: from ontology to relationship; from being to becoming; from description of ordered states to a description of dynamic processes; from an account of results to an account in terms of an evolutionary perspective. Very often the latter appears to suggest a description in terms of complexification focusing on the adaptive capabilities of a system as a whole. We find this in one form or another in most natural sciences as well as in the humanities, in physics as well as in sociology, ecology and economics. The mere fact of its occurrence

or its use does not tell us that this is the true and one and only description. Critics have pointed out that so far complexity research has promised much, but delivered little. Nevertheless, the concept of complexity gives us an interesting heuristic tool. Its application will hopefully throw new light on familiar elements of our discourse and bring into light forgotten or neglected elements.

2. A hermeneutics of complexity seems to promise an adequate understanding of interrelatedness and the interplay of order, and disorder, of universal and particular, global and local. The role played by irregularities and disturbances—whether in the very first moments of the universe or in the formation of galaxies or in the evolution of life—is a prominent and a fascinating one. To understand life and health as the just-right combination of order and disorder is indeed thought provoking. Life processes do not blindly follow deterministic schemes; they try to find the window between too much order and too much disorder. Too much order implies rigidity and sclerosis; too little order implies collapse and decay. Both of these states are lethal. Rigor mortis and decomposition are indeed marks of death.

3. However, we are faced with a fundamental difficulty: there is no valid definition of complexity, at least not apart from algorithmic definitions that are hard or impossible to apply to actual life processes. It seems to be part of the game of complexity to work without a simple definition.[45] Most helpful seems an inductive approach that describes complex systems as nonlinear, open, dynamic, emergent, and as poised between order and disorder. While some of these terms are rather elusive, others (nonlinear and open) have a more precise definition.

4. Yet, if there is supposed to be some reason to this hermeneutical attempt, we need at least a tentative description of complexity. I suggest as such: enough order that a pattern can be recognized, enough chaos that the pattern takes the shape of surprise, and an interplay of such a quality that suggests a description using terminology that applies to processes of life. Quantity alone does not count, and there needs to be a pattern, otherwise we would only have what physicist John Albright has called compoundity, or what Danish theologian Niels Henrik Gregersen calls complicatedness as the lowest level[46] of complexity.[47] Gregersen speaks about an increasing degree of self-organization from the level of complicated but predictable systems to the highest level of complexity in so called autopoietic (from Greek: autos/ self + poiein/make) systems. Whereas the behavior of complicated systems—the lowest level—is still deducible from the collective behavior of its constituents,[48] the self organizing or even self productive properties of autopoietic systems—the highest level in Gregersen's concept—transcend the possibilities of predicting outcomes.[49] This is indeed something new compared to more traditional philosophical understandings of complexity. If the recent research I refer to here is correct, it proves at least Ludwig Wittgenstein wrong, who stated what was and maybe still is a widely held understanding of complexity: "Every statement about complexes can be resolved into a statement about their constituents and into the propositions that describe the complexes completely."[50]

Why and how is such an interpretive effort that takes into account recent developments in both theology and science interesting for theology? I think the concept is attractive because it deals not only with retrospective, but also with possible outcomes or even possible worlds. The idea that God has created the world as self-productive or autopoietic offers an intriguing possibility of getting beyond the obsession with the questions of origins that marks the debates about creationism versus evolution. The focus on the autopoietic character of the world does not necessarily deny all concepts of God as designer, but it modifies them toward an inclusion of evolutionary concepts allowing for freedom and genuine novelty. Without being able to discuss this at length here, let me just suggest a couple of thoughts about how I can imagine complexity terminology to contribute constructively to an understanding of the concept of God.

In traditional teaching of Christianity there has been a tendency to associate God with the idea of simplicity. Most evidently, this happened in Thomas Aquinas who claims that God is utmost simplicity.[51] The above suggests that we change perspective and speak of God in terms of highest complexity. First of all, thinking of God in terms of complexity rather than simplicity has the advantage of making the concept of the Trinity more comprehensible. Advocates of the God of simplicity usually have difficulties with Trinitarian thinking. Aquinas made it a concept secondary to his basic explication of The One God, *De Deo Uno*. Newton, as already mentioned, actively disliked the idea of a Trinitarian God. In his opinion world peace would only be achieved at the expense of the complete abolition of Trinitarian models of God. At least since the 1980s however, we have seen a renaissance of Trinitarian thinking that has been vitalizing for Western theology. Feminist theologians have been much in favor of this change. They see in it a viable alternative to static and patriarchal God-talk, preoccupied with questions of order and hierarchy.

This development invites the question whether speaking of God and creation in terms of complexity is not more adequate today than holding to the category of simplicity. What would we gain? We would achieve new ways of understanding the interplay of free, individual agents, but also of the constrained and incomplete nature of those agents. Translated into talk about God it would imply something like: God is the well-spring of complex autopoietic systems. God lives a complex life, undergoes change, has freedom and grants freedom. Mutuality and relationship are marks of the divine. This new understanding would help to overcome anthropomorphic concepts of God that too easily turn into an anthropocentrism detrimental to the rest of creation. It would lead to increased openness to religious and cultural diversity.

In more traditional theological language, this would describe statements like: God chooses to be God *with* creation and not without it. God's omnipotence is qualified by God's granting freedom of participation to others. God's glory is revealed in, with, and under its opposite. Traditional problematic divine attributes such as immutability and impassibility can be revisited in an adequate way. Grace and freedom can be conceptualized without ruling out the notion of God's transformative power. However, complex systems are not stable, which poses a difficulty if we describe God as complexity. Would it make God contingent?[52] Or would it in the end reduce God to change without end? Complexity theory is certainly not the answer to all problems. But under the given circumstances, it seems to be at least a viable interpretive figure to be used with caution and critical discernment.

The Challenge from Postmodernisms

In this lecture I will argue that *postmodernism* in its most constructive form shares the best fruits of modernity, especially of the Enlightenment, while at the same time avoiding some of its most serious mistakes. In concluding these three lectures, I reflect on the three publics engaged in the dialogue between science and religion—academe, religious communities and societies—and offer an outline of constructive suggestions and critical observations concerning the future of this dialogue.

It would not surprise me if one or another scientist who has been with me thus far feels tempted to do something else during this last lecture. Many scientists work in a climate where feminism and postmodernism are counted as anti-science. It is difficult to understand this in the case of feminism, because there is enough evidence of scientific rigor in the discussion of feminist theories to disprove this belief. I hope I have been able to show something of that. However, when it comes to postmodernism I have less difficulty seeing why one would be worried on behalf of science. But these worries are healthy.

As an attempt to make this lecture less "wild," I will introduce what I want to say about postmodernism by taking a look at what a pre-postmodern philosopher might have to teach us about religion and science.

Nietzsche and Perspectivism

Postmodern philosophy seems to be more than a superficial trend that will be forgotten the day after tomorrow. In questioning at least two myths of modernity it raises issues that pertain to theology as well as to science. The two myths called into question by postmodernism are the myth of progress and the myth of secularization. Both of these presuppose that "the progressive advance toward modernity is supposed to be inseparable from a gradual movement away from religion."[1] In other words, much of modernity adheres to the axiom: Where modernism goes in, religion goes out. Cultural developments in the Western world during the 1990s have proven this axiom to be a myth (in the negative sense of the word), or at least, a grave simplification. The deconstruction of this myth has opened the way for new discussions of the question of God, as the work of leading philosophers like Jacques Derrida, Emanuel Lévinas and Jean-Luc Marion shows.

In order to understand these recent developments, we may wish to take a look at their roots. These date back at least to the 19th century. Friedrich Nietzsche's perspectivism—the denial of access to reality unmediated by interpretation—and his proclamation of the death of God are of vital importance for contemporary philosophy. Knowing that we cannot really look around our corner, Nietzsche points out that the acceptance of our perspective as a conditioned one has opened up a new infinity: "the world has once again become infinite to us: insofar as we cannot reject the possibility *that it includes infinite interpretations.*"[2] His late work, *On the Genealogy of Morals*, gives a lucid and vivid description of what perspectivism is and does. It deserves to be quoted at length:

> Henceforth, my dear philosophers, let us be on guard against the dangerous old conceptual fiction that posited a "pure, will-less, painless, timeless knowing subject"; let us guard against the snares of such contradictory concepts as "pure reason," "absolute spirituality," "knowledge in itself": these always demand that we should think of an eye that is completely unthinkable, an eye turned in no particular direction, in which the active and interpreting forces, through which alone seeing becomes seeing *something*,

> are supposed to be lacking; these always demand of the eye an absurdity and a nonsense. There is *only* a perspective seeing, *only* a perspective "knowing"; and the *more* affects we allow to speak about one thing, the *more* eyes, different eyes, we can use to observe one thing, the more complete will our "concept" of this thing, our "objectivity," be. But to eliminate the will altogether, to suspend each and every affect, supposing we were capable of this—what would that mean but to *castrate* the intellect?[3]

Nietzsche's perspectivism differs from intersubjectivity, a concept that is so important in science. Intersubjectivity shares with perspectivism the aspect of the many. Let as many as possible make the same experiment to strengthen its value of truth. There is a radical difference, however, in the desired result. Intersubjectivity strives for sameness; the ideal is that every observer arrives at exactly the same result. Nietzsche's perspectivism wants exactly the opposite. It strives for otherness, not for a unification of perspective. The latter would be what Nietzsche calls castration of the intellect. In the same vein, he says in *Twilight of the Idols*: "I distrust all systematicians and keep out of their way. The will to system is a lack of honesty."[4]

Already in his early work, *The Birth of Tragedy*, Nietzsche devotes some pages to thoughts about science and what he calls "the spirit of science." We need to note, however, that when Nietzsche speaks about science, he does not speak only about the natural sciences. He uses the German word, *Wissenschaft*, which includes both the natural sciences and the humanities.

Yet, he was well acquainted with the natural science of his time. It seems that Nietzsche learned about Darwinism early on.[5] His doctrine of *Übermensch*, though not directly dependent on Darwin, could neither be developed nor understood without any knowledge of Darwinism. "Nicht nur fort sollst du dich pflanzen, sondern hinauf!" [You shall not only re-produce yourself, but produce upward!][6]—this command of Zarathustra's can count as a valid expression of Nietzsche's interpretation of evolution. Nevertheless, Nietzsche criticizes the spirit of science for its belief in social engineering as a strategy to solve all of life's problems. In *The Birth of Tragedy* he points out that the un-Dionysian spirit of "the theoretical man"

> ... combats Dionysian wisdom and art, it seeks to dissolve myth, it substitutes ... a *deus ex machina* of its own, the god of machines and crucibles, that is, the powers of the spirits of nature recognized and employed in the service of a higher egoism; it believes that it can correct the world by knowledge, guide life by science, ..."[7]

In a later statement in *On the Genealogy of Morals*, Nietzsche almost seems to anticipate the ecological critique of science and technology as it was articulated during the latter half of the 20th century. Moreover, he relates the violation of the outer environment to a reductionist abuse of the inner sphere of human life:

> Our whole attitude toward nature, the way we violate her with the aid of machines and the heedless inventiveness of our technicians and engineers, is *hubris*; ... We violate ourselves nowadays, ... we nutcrackers of the soul, ... as if life were nothing but cracking nuts.[8]

Here, Nietzsche comes across as an early ecologist. He warns us from putting too much trust in science. He has discovered that the spirit of science as "the faith in the explicability of nature and in knowledge as a panacea" is not as affirmative of life as it sounds.[9] The people Nietzsche wants to see as scientists are people who are aware of the role of intuition, imagination and aesthetic choices. Nietzsche tells us that,

> ...great men, universally gifted, have contrived, with an incredible amount of thought, to make use of the paraphernalia of science itself, to point out the limits and the relativity of knowledge generally, and thus to deny decisively the claim of science to universal validity and universal aims. ... With this insight a culture is inaugurated that I venture to call a tragic culture. Its most important characteristic is that *wisdom takes the place of science as the highest end*—wisdom that ... seeks to grasp, with sympathetic feelings of love, the eternal suffering as its own.[10]

Nietzsche was convinced that he was very much ahead of his time, and listening to this quote seems to prove him right. This sounds more like a contemporary statement than a quote from a time that was yet to see the climaxes of both positivism and existentialism.

Nietzsche's message in *The Birth of Tragedy* is that we need to look at science in the perspective of an artist, but at art in the perspective of life.[11] Or, perhaps better, it is art that enables us to embrace chaos in ourselves and to give birth to a dancing star, as Nietzsche's Zarathustra states so famously and beautifully.[12] The spirit of science—understood as faith in the explicability of nature and in knowledge as a panacea—needs to be pushed to its limits. It cannot "heal the eternal wound of existence."[13] Only when these limits of science are reached will we realize the failure of its claim to universal validity, and we can expect art to play its redemptive and salvific role.[14]

Where science is taken seriously, it meets its own boundaries and gets stuck in pessimism, unless protected and rescued by art.[15] Phrased positively: the aesthetic provides a sense of tragic[16] realism that is able to save science from the excesses of positivism or scientism and religion from the decline into moralism. This insight will enhance wisdom.

The Death of God and Science

As is well known, Nietzsche proclaims the death of God. It is worth noting, however, that the death of God does not automatically imply an upswing for science. Nietzsche does not give any support to the popularized misunderstanding that increased rationality or expanding science speaks the death sentence over Christianity. From the very beginning, it is not lack of rationality that is the mistake of religion in general and Christianity in particular. What is wrong with Christianity is its lack of passion for life. Christianity is stuck with, as Nietzsche puts it, "life's nausea and disgust with life, ... dressed up as, faith in 'another' or 'better' life."[17] Yet, there are places in Nietzsche that seem to suggest a contradictory relationship between faith and science. In *Antichrist* we read that faith, as an imperative, is the veto against science; and Genesis 3, the story about the Fall, is addressed as the famous story about God's hellish fear of science.[18]

Nevertheless, both Christianity and science are targets of Nietzsche's sharp pencil, even if the attacks on science do not seem as fierce as those on religion. Christianity and science are dubious because they both cherish the same ideal, ascetism. In the third essay of *On the Genealogy of Morals*, Nietzsche attacks the ascetic ideal. The role of ascetism in Christian religion is quite obvious. Its role in science may be less visible, but it is equally important. Science and the ascetic ideal both rest on the same foundation, namely the belief that truth is inestimable and cannot be criticized. For this reason, scientists are far from being what they should be, namely free spirits. They are not free, because they still have faith in truth. The image of truth that shows up here is one of a deity demanding constant sacrifices. The unconditional will to truth, that is, faith in the ascetic ideal itself, is what captures scientists.[19] Therefore, any depreciation of the ascetic ideal—in Nietzsche's view highly desirable—also involves a depreciation of science.[20]

The alternative to look for would be, in Nietzsche's words, *Die fröhliche Wissenschaft*, "gay science" (also translated as "joyful wisdom"). Nietzsche's thought about the philosopher as a scholar can serve as an illustration of what he is aiming at. He tells us that "[m]aybe we philosophers [and it might equally apply to 'us theologians'] are all in a bad position regarding knowledge these days: science is growing, and the most scholarly of us are discovering that they know too little."[21] Yet, we should not be too depressed about that, because "[w]e *are* different from scholars, although we are inevitably also ... scholarly."[22] These insights should help us to strive for what Nietzsche likes to call a free spirit. Of such a free spirit he says

> I wouldn't know what the spirit of a philosopher might more want to be than a good dancer. For the dance is his ideal, also his art, and finally also his only piety, his "worship service [Gottesdienst]."[23]

Neither science nor religion has an easy match with Nietzsche. And neither of them has an easy match with religiosity or piety. Different forms of religious and spiritual practices can cause problems for religion and theology, the critical and self-critical study of religious traditions, as well as for science. Zarathustra is still called "the most pious of those who do not believe in God,"[24] and an aphorism about scientists in *Gay Science* bears the title *In what way we, too, are still pious.*[25]

Both religion and science enthusiastically affirm the will to truth. Yet, as Nietzsche has it, "[t]he will to truth, which will seduce us yet to many a risky venture... what manner of questions has this will to truth presented for us! What strange, wicked, questionable questions!"[26] Nietzsche realized that this very will to truth is deeply problematic:

> We see that science, too, rests on a faith; there is simply no 'presuppositionless' science. ... it is still a *metaphysical*

> *faith* upon which our faith in science rests— ... even we knowers of today, we godless antimetaphysicians, still take *our* fire, too, from the flame lit by the thousand-year old faith, the Christian faith which was also Plato's faith, that God is truth; that truth is divine ... [27]

And he goes on to conclude this aphorism with the words:

> But what if this [that truth is divine] were to become more and more difficult to believe, if nothing more were to turn out to be divine except error, blindness, the lie – if God himself were to turn out to be our longest lie? [28]

Obviously, Nietzsche himself cannot think of an alternative understanding of God either. God always remains opposite to error. However, exactly this dualism has occasionally been called into question. Under the headline "To Err Is Divine", Karl Peters suggests that we think of God as a process of creation and that one aspect of this process is mistake making, error making.[29] From this understanding of God, he concludes that "our creating new variations and then critiquing and evaluating them makes us, like Jesus and his followers, children of God."[30] I will not discuss the theological problems linked with such a position. My point is that we today discuss options that apparently were unavailable to Nietzsche. In his thought, science is dependent on the same metaphysical structure as Platonism, as religion, as Christianity. Hence, it shares in the preservation of what Nietzsche identifies as the same life-denying morality as Christianity. If the place left empty by the murdered God is filled by science, nothing is won at all. The cleansing must be much more radical than that. This Nietzschean suspicion against the modern ideals of language, knowledge and science has inspired late 20th century philosophers to see Nietzsche as an early postmodernist.

In the wake of Nietzsche, the concept of neutral, objective and universal knowledge has been thoroughly criticized. As historically and socially cultured beings, humans can only produce knowledge that is conditioned by a specific socio-cultural framework. It is extremely problematic, not to say impossible, to define timeless criteria for truth and rationality, which does not mean that we have to abandon notions of truth and rationality altogether. We are not asked to succumb to resignation or skepticism but to acknowledge the limits of rationality more honestly than modern thinking used to do.

Postmodern philosophy implies the definite fall from innocence for scientific knowledge. Who is a good scientist then? What is good science? According to Nietzsche, its foremost mark should be the affirmation of life: the will to being, the great 'Yes' to life with all its changes, with pain and suffering, but also with ecstasy and a sense of the tragic. That is "Gay Science," a science that in spite of all caveats has a good eye for physics:

> We ... want to *become who we are*—human beings who are new, unique, incomparable, who give themselves laws, who create themselves! To that end we must become the best students and discoverers of everything lawful and necessary in the world: we must become *physicists* in order to be creators in this sense— while hitherto all valuations and ideals have been built on *ignorance* of physics or in *contradiction* to it. So, long live physics! And even more long live what *compels* us to it—our honesty![31]

This passage represents an interesting combination of modern and postmodern thought. It anticipates postmodern thought in advocating that knowledge is *poiesis* rather than *mimesis* or *anamnesis*, and it clings to modern morality by affirming the compelling role of honesty. On the one hand, Nietzsche advocates self-creation and projection, and on the other hand, he promotes honest observation of a built-in lawfulness. Are we creators of reality or products of nature's laws? It seems, as one of Nietzsche's biographers has pointed out, that "Nietzsche lived in the wrenching tension between two such visions—one of the great cosmic game and the other of power as *'causa prima.'*"[32] The same biographer contends that Nietzsche, the critic of the metaphysical 'world behind,' nevertheless was being seduced by scientific worlds behind.[33]

But could a man who over and over again refers to dance as the supreme expression of life be anything else than that? The oscillation between secure terrain and the abyss of uncertainty is mandatory for the Nietzschean dancer. Life cannot thrive without tragedy and without sensing more than it knows. Yet, at the same time it is drawn to safe knowledge. It wants clarity, but woe if it finds that clarity. When everything is clear, the rest is disappointment. Without the attraction of the enigmatic, of chaos, life would be over. As much as Nietzsche rejected idealism,[34] there remains a reversed idealism in his apotheosis of life as pleasure and passion, as agony and ecstasy. His early reflections on science stood under the motto of Apollo and Dionysus with a fraternal union of the two deities as the highest goal.[35] In his later works, he more or less forgets about Apollo. What remains is Dionysus. The scales weigh down on the side of "the fair frenzy of artistic enthusiasm," seen by the eye that is granted "the pleasure of gazing into the Dionysian abysses."[36]

From Nietzsche to Postmodernism

I can identify with the scientist who says "Let them tell me that it's all construction, but the technological applications of my science are still very real," or "Let them believe that it is all a matter of interpretation and contextuality, but 2+2 still makes 4, whether you are in Goshen or Baghdad, in Calcutta or Reykjavik, in Jerusalem or Chicago, on Earth or on the moon." We cannot reduce everything to otherness and particularity; there are, after all, things left that are marked by sameness and universality. We must affirm this even though, as is well known, respect for what is other and care for what is particular are the "good guys" of postmodern thought, while reduction of diversity to sameness and preoccupation with universal systems are somehow the "bad guys." Paradoxically, the universalism attacked by postmodern and postcolonial critique sometimes reappears in the critique itself, as a tool of the very critique that tries to unmask the oppressiveness of the universalism of the other(s). Critique of universalism has to struggle with the risk of becoming universalizing itself.

Of course, 2+2 makes 4 on the Indian countryside as well as in Greenland. But as an Indian scholar recently told me in a conversation: "You know, we really appreciate that some Western missionaries said: Unless you send not only the boys but also the girls, we will close this school. That was fine. Nevertheless, *how* they taught our children that 2+2 makes 4, the system they used, the examples they chose, the applications they trained, they were not ours."

We have to realize that all theory is value-laden. Data do not simply speak for themselves. There is no innocent communication. Scientific theory also communicates values, sometimes in a very subtle way. Francis Bacon's optimism that "[g]enuine truth is uniform and self-reproducing"[37] seems naïve today.

Constructive Postmodernism

In its most constructive form, postmodernism offers a way between the Scylla of boundless relativism and the Charybdis of rigorous non-ambiguity, of totalization, of reduction to sameness. Actually, constructive postmodernism shares some of the best features of

Enlightenment thinking: Postmodern thought can be understood in the same way as Enlightenment thought—not as the construction of permanent principles, but as the establishment of the principles of permanent critique. I think I have support for this point by no less than the one who has been called the prophet of deconstruction and the incarnation of postmodernism, Jacques Derrida. In the words of John Caputo, one of the foremost interpreters of French postmodernism in the U.S.A.: "Derrida would describe himself not as a postmodern, but as a man of the Enlightenment, albeit of a *new* Enlightenment, one that is enlightened about the Enlightenment and resists letting the spirit of the Enlightenment freeze over into dogma."[38]

Postmodernism does not necessarily say that everything is construction, but it argues that everything comes along with constructions. "Science does not descend from the sky like a god to save us, but neither are we just making it up as we go along."[39] There is a solid middle path to walk between the extremes of rigid rationality and fuzzy relativism.

Regarded in this way, modernism and postmodernism seem closer to each other than one might have originally thought. René Descartes' famous *cogito, ergo sum* (I think, therefore I am), appears to have a respectable partner in a postmodern *dubito, ergo sum* (I doubt, therefore I am). As Descartes invoked God as the guarantor of the coherence of perception, so even postmodernists seem to invoke guarantors. More or less surprisingly, some of them, Jacques Derrida, Gianni Vattimo and John Caputo, turn to God in one way or another.[40] Others, like Emmanuel Lévinas, see the guarantee in the face of the other person as the place where transcendence and ethics meet.[41] The ethical demand expressed in the face of the Other/the You is of divine dignity.

In my view, the continuity between modernity and postmodernity is far greater than the discontinuity between the two phenomena. There are, no doubt, significant dissimilarities, especially concerning the notions of universalism, totalization and sameness. But the word postmodernism itself, with its connotation of a linear chronology, is perfectly modern. "What then is the postmodern?" asks Jean-François Lyotard, and answers, "It is undoubtedly part of the modern."[42] We can see still greater similarities, especially if we, as I suggested above, choose to interpret the critiques of the Enlightenment (such as the Kantian critiques of pure and practical reason and of judgment) not as the establishment of permanent principles, but as the principles of permanent critique.

In spite of all the differences between modernity and postmodernity, even postmodern thinking in its most constructive shape embraces the message of the parable of the rings as presented by Gotthold Ephraim Lessing in the Enlightenment play *Nathan the Wise*: The noble competition of the best candidates for truth.[43] The story about the rings runs like this:

An exceedingly precious and beautiful ring has been passed down from generation to generation in a family. This ring has the secret power of making the owner loved by God and people, if the owner is mindful of this promise. The rule says that the father, before his death, ought to give the ring to his most beloved son (there are no mothers and daughters in the story). The ring has now come upon a father of three sons. As death draws near, the father realizes that he loves his sons equally and thus cannot decide which of his sons should receive the ring. Finally, he has an artist make two more rings, identical in appearance to the ring that carries the wonderful promise. No one, not even the father himself, can tell the difference between the rings by looking at them. Secretly, he gives each son a ring. Of course, confusion abounds after the father's death. Which one is the true ring? Who is going to be the true leader, loved by God and people? How can they find the truth? The judge they have called in conjectures that the father had wanted to put an end to the tyranny of the one and only ring, that is, the one and only truth. Hence, the only thing the three ring owners can do is to outdo each other in being good. The judge tells them to strive for tolerance and love without prejudice.

In Lessing's play, the father symbolizes God and the three rings symbolize the three Abrahamic religions; and in this sense the parable is as topical today as ever. I think, however, that the model of noble competition can also apply to the question of truth in our postmodern situation.

In this sense of noble competition, postmodern critique is not as radical as it might appear. Actually, it has much in common with what physicist and Nobel laureate Max Born so elegantly stated in his Nobel lecture from 1954, at a time when postmodernism was hardly spoken of:

> I believe that ideas such as absolute certitude, absolute exactness, final truth etc. are figments of the imagination which should not be admissible in any field of science. On the other hand, any assertion of probability is either right or wrong from the standpoint of the theory on which it is based. This *loosening of thinking* seems to me to be the greatest blessing which modern science has given to us. For the belief in a single truth and in being the possessor thereof is the root cause of all evil in the world.[44]

Postmodern critique has trained us in healthy suspicion toward the big singulars of our cultures and inspires us to experiment with plural forms. However, embracing the creativity of play and plurality is not the same as ignoring rational structures. Quite the reverse, it is depending on rationality, yet offering more. The postmodern quest, as I understand it, is not a quest for less rationality but for more than rationality. "More than rationality" would mean an understanding of rationality beyond its merely epistemological character. It takes into account the contextuality of rationality and its interrelatedness with emotions, intuition, imagination and various contingencies. It is also critically aware of the fact that rationality tends to carry ideological connotations that privilege certain ways of knowing over others. This "more than rationality" does not say that causes do not matter, but it suggests that there is more to the whole picture than an explanation in terms of A causes B.

At least two outcomes of the Human Genome Project seem to point in the same direction. There are only a third as many genes as anticipated, and junk DNA (DNA that does not code for proteins) does not seem to be junk after all. Neither of these findings makes sense in a framework that permits only a 1:1 correspondence between cause and effect. Rather, these findings suggest that we look in the direction of interaction and relatedness more than we have done before. It is not just that A causes B, but it is also about a web of relations that brings about complex developments. In a similar vein, instead of trying to describe autopoietic systems, maybe we should rather be looking for communio-poietic systems (if this linguistic mixture of Latin and Greek is allowed).

Postmodernism does not begin with what makes up a system—with what knits things together. As such, it questions the status of a Theory of Everything as the "natural," ultimate goal of science. Rather, it prefers to look for ruptures and disturbances and asks what they reveal. That is what deconstruction is about:

> A deconstruction is an exhibition of complexity and hidden tensions which demonstrates that beneath the calm surface of unity a thing puts forth there lies a multiplicity of competing elements, that beneath the reassuring look of certitude and knowledge there is restlessness and undecidability. Underneath the look of seamless continuity there are ruptures and interruptions and disruptive discontinuities. ... This is not to say that there is no truth or tradition, but

rather that truth and tradition and continuity are not what they say they are....[45]

We could say that deconstruction is a strategy that was already successfully applied by quantum physicists in coping with the frustration of the discovery that quantum theory turned the great expectations of progress in atomic theory into resignation. The understanding of what this rupture revealed was key to the success of quantum theory, as Niels Bohr suggested in a 1929 lecture.[46]

Postmodernism is not happy with looking at abstract reason only. It keeps asking what the significance of embodied reason is. Let my try to express this with an image. Postmodernism, in the benevolent reading that I suggest, does not diminish the exact knowledge about the molecular components of a drug, but it claims that the knowledge of how anticipated effects of the drug interact with such semi-exact or subjective factors as a person's age, body weight, sex and gender, race, mental state and belief system is equally respectable and necessary. This is not saying that these factors were not considered at all before 'post-modern prescribers' entered the stage (remember that this is only an image). It is more about trying to make the point that factors like these previously tended to represent secondary knowledge situated on the very fringes of core science. In a postmodern framework, they would be more likely regarded as a core part of adequate knowledge.

Postmodernism is not satisfied with looking at the self only. The (embodied) self is also a communal self. Consequently, postmodernism claims that any body of knowledge and every social institution are marked by a call from the other, a call that it either suppresses or encourages. This constitutes the basis for the claim of postmodernism that ethics overcomes ontology.[47]

In the benevolent reading I suggest, postmodernism can help the science-and-religion dialogue to keep out of the ditches of either divinizing or demonizing one or both of science and religion.

Commitment to listen to the voice of the other nourishes the hope that insights from postmodern thinking might help to bring about a more wholesome future for more people. However, for that to happen, postmodernism needs to break through the walls of individualism and get rid of the flavor of intellectual luxury that has surrounded it for quite a while.

It may rightly be argued that all three challenges that I have addressed in these lectures are variations of only one theme, namely hermeneutics in a broad sense. Because feminism is so broad and diverse a movement, I think it is highly justified to treat it as a special issue. The continuity between hermeneutics and postmodernism is rather explicit. It is not pure coincidence that John Caputo entitled two of his books *Radical Hermeneutics* and *More Radical Hermeneutics*. Yet, the specifics of postmodern discourse also provide reasons for a separate treatment, especially in its relation to science.

I do not claim that I have presented you with an exhaustive presentation of these three challenges. Much more could be done with each of them. However, at this point, let me summarize where these thoughts have taken us:

What I have tried to show is that contexts, presuppositions, biases and interpretations have always mattered. However, awareness and the critical reflection about *how* they matter have varied throughout history. The 20th century has seen significant contributions toward an understanding of what hermeneutics is and how it works. I have argued that the critique of the modern concept of sameness[48] by the postmodern concept of otherness does not pose a threat to science. However, it implies a significant challenge that needs to be addressed for the sake of science and its beneficial consequences for all creation. Affirming this appears to be a way of not getting lost between the Scylla of boundless pluralism and the Charybdis of reduction to sameness. We need a permanent deconstructive process of ideals, cultures and ideologies. We are urged to be open to an emphasis on otherness or radical alterity—what Derrida has called "le tout autre." This tells us that totalization or immanentism, staying inside one and only one frame of reference, is no longer a hermeneutical virtue. It was once—in the natural sciences and the humanities as well as in theology. Staying within one system and using sameness as an interpretive code was a scientific ideal as well as a theological one. The only possible alternatives thought of were deus ex machina solutions (a god miraculously descending from the skies), which are acceptable in Greek drama, but seemed deeply unacceptable in terms of a rational worldview for modern people, as, for example, Nietzsche made clear to us. This critique of metaphysical constraints on science had its equivalence in the affirmation of immanentism in theology, most famously in the shape of the God-is-dead theologies of the 1960s. At that time, immanentism appeared to be the wonder drug against metaphysical frameworks that had become obsolete.

Today's critique runs in a different direction. Without spoiling what we gained from the Enlightenment, we need to think of ways to avoid an immanentism that believes in watertight systems and explanations in terms of sameness. It needs to be avoided because it is typical of fanatic and nationalist ideologies, and because it is prone to xenophobic violence. Instead of this, we need transcendence, understood as the search for connectedness with the other (or the search for the understanding of complexity, if you prefer that terminology). It is the encounter with the face of the other, at least according to Lévinas, that makes us feel our radical ethical responsibility and hinders us from hiding beyond closed identities. In other words, it is the encounter with the other that makes us truly human. It is the encounter with the other that turns suspicion from a vice into an art, and makes good interpretation and understanding possible—in religion as well as in science.

With these thoughts in mind, I want to conclude by sharing with you some of the ideas I have concerning the future of the dialogue between religion and science.

Looking into the future of the religion-and-science dialogue

My presupposition is that the science-religion dialogue addresses basically three publics that partly overlap, namely academe, religious communities, and societies. As an invitation to further discussion, let me briefly share some ideas of what is required to respond to the needs of these three publics.

In the *academic world*, we need to engage younger scholars and—in an international perspective—take advantage of smaller, younger, upcoming universities and colleges with fresh resources; these institutions often have less compartmentalization and more interdisciplinarity at the core of their teaching and research profile than traditional universities have. It should no longer be the case that a scientist's interest in questions of ethics, world-view and religion is regarded as detrimental to his or her career. Interdisciplinary engagement should be a realistic opportunity for scientists and theologians well before the time they approach retirement. If it is a realistic expectation that this dialogue makes better scientists and even better science, better theologians and even better theology, and if we expect both to contribute to a world with more justice and more peace, then some things should change in the academic world.

We also need to discuss the question whether or how religion-and-science should develop into a discipline in its own right. Should it be institutionalized as a kind of epistemic community,[49] or should scholars rooted and active in their own specialties pursue it in the form of side projects or ad-hoc conversations? I tend to favor the second option, because the direct involvement at the places where discipline-specific research actually happens remains crucial to successful dialogue.

In terms of *religious communities*, two related strands of dialogue need to be developed: conceptual worldview thinking and ethical questions. It goes without saying that it is desirable to do this ecumenically, interfaith or at least multifaith. Religious communities should not underestimate the promise of a process where proponents of different religious traditions meet not only to discuss questions of faith with each other, but also to discuss science and technology. There is much to gain in terms of ecumenism and interfaith relationships from such a dialogue.

It should also be a joint project to fight anti-intellectualism in religious communities. As a candidate for a promising common platform for conversation, I suggest further exploration of the concept of wisdom. How does (scientific) knowledge relate to wisdom? On this topic we can expect valuable contributions from many religions and denominations. In the Christian sphere, Eastern Orthodox theologians seem to have been the best stewards of the concept of wisdom. Thinking especially of Sergii Bulgakov,[50] the sophiological tradition is controversial enough to be exciting, and thinking of various religious traditions, it is common enough to be constructive. In combination with the thought-tradition linked to the life and work of Pavel Florensky, this topic can bring something new and longed-for to the dialogue that for so long has been dominated by Western Christianity.[51] In recent years, Western theology has been increasingly open to wisdom thought, as shown for example in works by Jürgen Moltmann,[52] inspired by Judaism, Elizabeth Johnson,[53] inspired by the scriptural Sophia-tradition, and by Celia Deane-Drummond,[54] applied to theology-and-biology. In my view, it will also be healthy and helpful to link Western thoughts about divine *kenosis* (usually translated as the self-emptying of God), as a popular concept in the science-and-religion dialogue, to the strengths of the Eastern Orthodox concept of *theosis* (usually translated as deification).

In terms of *societies* it should be a shared interest to increase both science and religious literacy. In many countries and societies it is an urgent task to keep public discourse alive in the face of an increasing privatization of politically significant questions.

In a societal perspective, we also need to address the issue of instrumentalization of religion, especially concerning an expanding area of research. We need a rigorous examination of the methods used when scholars study the health effects of religion and prayer. These studies need to be seen in the context of societies that face an aging population and the problem of increasing costs for health care and pensions. They require a theological analysis of the underlying assumptions and of the intended applications as well as a discussion about unintended possible applications of the results. "An Apple a Day Keeps the Doctor Away" makes me smile. "A Service a Day Keeps the Doctor Away"[55] seems to me deeply problematic.

Finally, from the viewpoint of societal implications, we need to move beyond the implicit division into science-theology/religion on the one hand, and technology-ethics on the other. For ordinary, practical people, this is a highly artificial separation. In terms of social responsibility, there is no such division. Most of the burning issues, like questions of anthropology, artificial intelligence, stem cell research, therapeutic and reproductive cloning, reproductive rights, overpopulation issues, and physician-aided suicide, transcend this polarization anyway.

What Bacon calls "a mixture of religion and science"[56] is indeed not a good idea. The opposite isn't either, as the anecdote told about the pious Michael Faraday and his two keys suggests.[57] A toothless harmony is as bad as a watertight separation. Science-and-religion is certainly not about smoothing out all the discontinuities, forgetting the depth of the abysses and the height of the mountains yet to climb. None of this can be done without a body whose muscles are kept in just the right tension. It is my hope that the community of scholars in religion-and-science will form bodies that keep up what the Greek called *eu-tonos*—a beneficial or salutary tension—as a necessary condition for an energetic and fruitful relationship.

Sunday Worship

Minding God and the Mind and Heart of God
Jeremiah 31:31-34
John 12:20-33

A mother was preparing pancakes for her sons, Kevin, age 5, and Ryan, age 3. The boys began to argue over who would get the first pancake. Their mother saw the opportunity for a moral lesson. If Jesus were here, *he* would say, "Let my *brother* have the first pancake. I can wait." There was only the slightest of pauses before Kevin turned to his younger brother, and said to him, "Ryan, you be Jesus."

Ah, children. Their antics so often serve as teachers to us about ourselves. One of the reasons it works that way, of course, is that we can chuckle at them as though we're not really looking at ourselves at all. They're little; they're cute; they haven't learned about delay of gratification or about taking turns or even about taking care of your friends. Once they're grown they'll know better—like us. But when we're a little more honest, of course, the truth sinks in. It really is us that those stories reflect. Our laughter is a response to an unpleasant recognition of our own self-deceptions. That apparent invitation to another to be a follower of Jesus too often serves our own self-interest. Our attempts to help others become disciples of Christ too often merely mask our own self-centeredness, our needs to manage the world so that we come out okay.

The well-meaning mother in that story has the lesson of self-sacrifice partially right, of course, if somewhat simplistically so. "Those who love their life lose it, and those who hate their life in this world will keep it for eternal life." These words of Jesus are some of the most familiar words in the Gospels—even to those outside the context of Christian faith. They appear in recognizable form in all four Gospels, though here the writer of John sets them in the context of Jesus' Passion, emphasizing his willingness to sacrifice his own life for the cause of the Truth he proclaimed. We recall these words less than two weeks before we will once again remember Jesus' ignominious death on the cross; they deepen our understanding of what that death was all about. The Christ of John was troubled by what lay ahead of him, but instead of a soul struggle in the Garden of Gethsemane this Jesus understands the pivotal nature of what was to come—that it was to be the fulfillment of his mission in the world. This was indeed the fullness of time— the purpose for which John's Jesus had come into the world.

They are some of the most memorable words of Jesus—and they may also be some of the most troublesome, particularly at this point in global history. This directive of Jesus is not unique to Christianity of course. Promises of rewards for martyrdom have long been used to motivate believers to sacrifice of life in pursuit of a cause that transcends them. Such notions supported the men who commandeered airplanes and carried out the disastrous work of September 11, 2001. Similar understandings continue to motivate suicide bombings around our troubled world and, in ways that deepen the inevitable tragedies of war, such ideas have given cause to U.S. soldiers to shoot innocent men, women and children out of fear that they too may be bent on destruction of others by destroying themselves. Undoubtedly members of our armed forces may be rehearsing this passage even as we speak – all in attempts to make sense of being sent to war and the threat to their own lives. "Private Ryan, you be Jesus."

In a tragic twist of meaning, over the course of history some have heard Jesus' words as exalting death in the service of Christ. Out of that understanding, some have sought out death as a guaranteed, free one-way ticket to the highest levels of heaven rather than seeing death as a risk that is run by those who first and foremost sought out and spoke the Truth. "Go directly to heaven, do not pass 'Go,' do not collect $200." This one turns our story upside down. It's now as though heaven becomes that coveted first pancake and glimpsing the rewards that appear now in easy reach, Ryan signs himself up—"I'll be Jesus!"

As if that weren't enough of a problem for this text, in recent years we've become painfully aware that messages of self-sacrifice register differently for women than they do for men. In many cultures, notably including our own, self-denial in deference to the needs of others has been the default position expected of women. Self-interest has too often been disallowed as a legitimate goal. If pride and self-aggrandizement have been the sins of men, devaluing of self is now seen as the sin of choice for women. As a society for centuries we've been positioning ourselves at the front of the pancake line. "Women, you be Jesus."

And all those contemporary problems piled on top of the ever-present tasks of exegesis. We know that we must carefully work to understand the settings of these ancient words and avoid interpreting them too easily in the terms of today. We must first learn what they would have meant in the day and age in which they were spoken before we can hope to interpret them with integrity here and now. Given all those hurdles, why would anyone grapple with such texts unless they were forced to by a lectionary that calls them up every three years? Why not choose something less troubling, or less ambiguous? What's a preacher to do?

I've long lived by the premise that real preachers don't avoid difficult texts, as tempting as that can be. For we all know that the Scriptures can afflict the comfortable just as certainly as they can comfort the afflicted. So here we go.

Biblical scholar colleagues have taught me that it helps to look on either side of such a central passage to tease out the depths of meaning of the text. And the Gospel writer is helpful here, for his Jesus introduces this passage with the nearly-as-familiar image of the grain of wheat that falls into the earth and dies. This is a death with a purpose—to bring forth much more wheat. Without the death of the seed, no more wheat will appear. Without wheat to make bread, no one will be fed. Jesus' death would lead to the emerging of the Kin-dom of God that was already present in him. A new community would form around the crucified and risen Christ that would not only carry on the message of God's love, but would extend it to all peoples of the earth. So in this context the passage tells us something critical about the early church's understanding of the unique meaning of Jesus' death.

When we look at what follows these famous verses we learn even more about this deep connection between Jesus' death and the community to which that death would give birth. Jesus predicts that in being lifted up he would draw all people unto himself; that has much more to do with the creation of new community than it has to do with personal fulfillment. So that's about Jesus.

But what about us? Can five-year-old Kevin say something to us as well—something like "You be Jesus?" Indeed the story has much to say to our self-understanding as children of God as well. For whatever else it may have meant to Jesus, it was not his own well-being that motivated his willingness to suffer the consequences of truth-telling. It was no personal heavenly destination that by itself drew him unwaveringly forward. It was rather a vision of God's full presence in the world, reconciling peoples of the world to each other and to God. Whatever else motivates our willingness to pay the cost of discipleship, it is not personal glory. It has something rather to do with self-transcendence, a willingness to expend life in the service of God's reign.

It is here that Jeremiah raises a hand and asks for the microphone. For he has something important to add to the discussion. Jeremiah hears the word of the Lord proclaiming "I will make a new covenant with the house of Israel and the house of Judah." It is to be unlike anything God's children have experienced before, including the covenant that brought them out of Egypt—and sadly a covenant they had been unable to honor. Jeremiah understood that obedience to God was no easy accomplishment—history was replete with stories of the failures of the children of God to live up to God's law. And he understood that was so because the law was outside of them so that they could never measure up.

But Jeremiah saw another way. He foresaw a time when God would write the entirety of the law on their hearts. Now the law would be within them, and the passion of the people would be the love and service of God. And the result? "I will be their God, and they shall be my people." Reconciliation between God and God's people would at long last become reality. The will of God's people would be identical to God's will. It would be a world in which human beings no longer need to correct or teach each other, or even remind each other of God's love. We will know it and live it without being told. And that is the very new covenant that Christians believe Jesus instituted in his life, death and resurrection.

But wait a minute; that can't be right. Jeremiah couldn't possibly have meant that, could he? Just look around. Justice is far from automatic in a world where people still go to war—invading nations who have not threatened them and whose military might is so limited that the entire nation can be virtually destroyed in two weeks. It's hard to give much credit to Jeremiah's vision when we see the continued oppression of whole groups of people by the wealthy and powerful, when violence in our cities spills over into the country, and where state-sanctioned murders become so routine that it is the states that *don't* execute people that make the news. There are occasional glimpses of justice and love of God, but they sadly seem to be the exception rather than the rule. Can Jeremiah have missed it by such a wide margin?

So once again we are confronted with the theological counterpart to that sign of emotional maturity—delay of gratification. Jeremiah's vision is of one of that is not yet, but of what is yet to be. It is a vision of a world to which we can aspire, while we live in the meantime in the shadow of its incompleteness. We can believe in that world, and it can lure us forward toward it, but we must also wait for it. So how shall we then live?

There's a clue hidden in the Jeremiah passage that we might miss if we're not paying close attention. His vision is one in which teaching, correcting and reminding are no longer necessary—the image and love of God and God's law are so intimately a part of us that accountability to each other is not required. But in the meantime—until that day truly arrives—Jeremiah's words point us once again to the communal reality of our life together. We need each other; we cannot survive in these in between times without communities of faith that support and challenge us, that hold us, and hold us accountable, to our faith.

Could it be that we Ryans need our older brothers to remind us regularly whose we are? Could it be that we really are to be "little Christs" to each other—to live out the missions to which we have been called? Could it just be...?

Discussions

Discussions followed the public lectures on hermeneutics and feminism and the internal lecture on postmodernism. There was a brief open microphone discussion following the first lecture on hermeneutics. However, this was not recorded.

The internal discussions were all recorded. There has been extensive editing of the questions and comments of the participants. The answers and comments of Professor Jackelén have been edited only slightly in order to keep all of her thoughts in complete form for the reader. Professor Jackelén's answers to the questions were, almost uniformly, extensive and detailed.

The topics discussed have been ordered and do not necessarily appear as they did in the conference. The discussion on Saturday morning, which followed the lecture on hermeneutics, strayed considerably from the single topic. The discussion of Saturday afternoon following the lecture on feminism dealt almost uniformly with feminism and the principal part of the discussion is under a single heading. The discussion of postmodernism on Sunday morning stayed on the single topic of postmodernism. For this last discussion only sub-headings were added to help the reader. The discussion is otherwise essentially intact.

The topics of the discussions are organized here under the following headings and sub-headings.

Development of Science
Muslims
Western Christianity
Progress in Science and in Religion

Time and Eternity
Doctoral Dissertation
Purgatory and Mansions
Christology
City of God

Language
Language and Mathematics
Complexity and Chaos

Feminism
Gender and Science
Women in Science
Women and Male Images
Women and Competition

Postmodernism
Defined
Truth and Judgment
Present and Future
Hermeneutics
Eastern Orthodoxy
Epistemology and Brain Science
Theologians

Development of Science

Muslims

Speaker 1: There are Muslim scholars who claim that Islam is very much the best of modern science. According to Muslim apologists I have read tradition Muhammad himself holds that you should seek knowledge even if you have to go as far as China. Muslim apologists say that Islam has never had any problem with evolution, for example. And yet when one looks at the world of Islam, there's a certain kind of ideological control that discourages the idea of fresh investigation.

In contrast there are two very respected British scholars on Islam, Sir Hamilton Gibb[1] and William Montgomery Watt[2] who claim that in the Islamic world, there is the concept that there exists only given quantity of knowledge. All knowledge is already present. The only question is how much any one individual can master. A notable Muslim scholar of the 10th Century of the Common Era (Ibn Taimiyya), who claimed that the gates to of ijtihad are closed, also put this idea forth. That is the door to further interpretation of Islamic truth or any truth is really closed and all that remains is to master the knowledge that we have been given.

The western Christian tradition has a different concept based, it seems, on a salvation history. The origin of science is the western Christian tradition. And, even though there is a checkered history between religion and science, science is still a child of western Christianity. In salvation history is the idea of progress, and the revelation that we have in Christ is not a final one, the way Islam views the revelation through Muhammad as final and closed. In other words the Christian theological vision is shaping science at the same time that scientific discoveries are dialectically changing of theology.

Antje Jackelén: This has always intrigued me. Why did what we call modern science emerge from the Christian west? We know that Muslim culture was flourishing during the Middle Ages. Why didn't it happen there? I don't know whether there's a single answer to that question. Some people claim that political circumstances prohibited further development of the Muslim culture in Spain, or that war influenced this. But it seems to me that external factors are not the only answer. There is, as you indicate, something internal in the tradition.

Muslims obviously were engaged in scientific activities and in research. Research in the Christian tradition was partly, and cosmology particularly, motivated by the fact that we needed to find a fixed date for Easter. But in Islam you have to fix the date for Ramadan, so there are parallels.

Modern Muslim scholars who are interested in the dialog in science and religion often point out that there is no fundamental difficulty in Islam that would prevent your doing science. They want to show that a good scientist is also a good Muslim. But it is value guided. For instance, in biotechnology, or methods for assisted reproduction, the value of the family and certain family values, are guideposts.

You mentioned evolution and that Muslims claim that there is no objection to evolution. It's my impression that evolution is not a key concept in discussions between Islam and science. One should also note that questions about evolution and creationism are not characteristic of the dialogue between Christianity and science. Such questions are characteristic of much of what is going on in this country. But these are not issues in most of the dialogue that is going on in other parts of the world between Christianity and science. We all tend to think that what is characteristic of our concept is more universal than it actually is.

If you ask what it was in Christianity that stimulated scientific research, I would point to two issues. One is creation theology,

Discussions 87

and the other is eschatology. If humans are created in the image of God and if rationality is a significant part of that image of God, then we should use our rationality to find out how this creation actually works. So there is a stimulus for scientific research to be found in the tradition of the two books (Scripture and the Book of Nature) and in the belief that we see the face of the Creator in the world. Eschatology entails a working towards the realization of the reign of God, which involves making the world a better place. That implies science and technology.

Both main branches of Western Christianity, Roman Catholicism and the Reformation Churches, have the concept that knowledge increases and that you can obtain new insights. In Catholicism there is the notion that ongoing revelation can occur. We can develop new doctrines. So then we must be able to obtain new knowledge. We also know that the Reformation started out in part as an intellectual movement, and has always had a connection to intellectualism. So there are significant reasons why one would get engaged with scientific study.

It is different with Eastern Orthodoxy. Russian Orthodoxy particularly has had a stronger focus on spirituality. In Western Christianity, monasteries have been centers of culture and intellectual endeavor. In Russia, however, monasteries were centers of spirituality, and not centers of secular knowledge. If we can place spirituality on one side of the table and intellectualism on the other, we can see that there is a difference in the approaches of Western and Eastern Christian traditions. Not only was theology done in Western monastic libraries but other research as well. In the Eastern tradition there was a clear statement, "That doesn't belong here; that's inferior." In Western churches, often the brightest sons were sent to be priests. In Russian Orthodoxy, that was not always the case. Rather it was those who were able to sing who were sent to be priests. And the brightest ones were often destined to do something else. So there's a slightly different attitude here, which is one of the reasons, I think, that we have so far not been very good at actually getting Eastern Orthodox Christians to play a vital part in the dialogue between religion and science. It's going to change, I believe, but so far there has been little motion.

Western Christianity

Speaker 2: I would like to comment on the development of science in the Western world. I think there are many factors that come into play, one of which was the development of commerce within the Mediterranean. The fact that people of different cultures came together and influenced one another aided in the development of science. Also, there was a fragmentation in the latter part of the Middle Ages and the rediscovery of Greek philosophy, with new emphasis upon man. This shifted the focus of interest, and gave us a new view of what the world was like. In Italy, during a period of 50 to 60 years, three poets exemplify the shift. Dante is considered to be a man standing with his feet above ground and looking up to heaven. Petrarch, about 20-30 years after Dante, had his with his feet underground, but still looking up to heaven. And then the third one that came a few years later, Boccaccio who was really with his feet on the ground and looking around the earth. At this point with the emphasis upon man, the discovery of things related to man became more important.

Antje Jackelén: You're perfectly right about the various factors, which are, at least in part, interdependent. You mentioned commercialism. The French historian Jacques Le Goff, pointed out that the rediscovery and further development of the idea of purgatory actually had a significant impact on commercialism and capitalism. He argued that before purgatory was an option, moneylenders would definitely go to hell. There was no option for them. And, therefore money lending was a very, very bad business. But purgatory has only one exit, and that is to paradise. So if the moneylender goes to purgatory, that's still bad, but eventually the moneylender will end up in paradise. That, he says, really helped capitalism get a start and with that commerce and, in a sense, probably also scientific inquiry. I don't know whether that theory is correct, but it's interesting and it makes you think of the way in which theological changes, shifts, and innovations, actually have consequences far from their origin. That has, of course, been true throughout history.

Progress in Science and in Religion

Speaker 3: Last night you spoke of progress in science and progress in religion. I find it not difficult to identify progress in science. Progress in theology seems to have much more of a patchwork quality. I'm wondering what are the standards by which you define progress in science and progress in theology.

Antje Jackelén: Obviously my notion of progress was a pretty open one. What I spoke of was not a strong definition of progress. I was speaking of something in the direction of development, of change. I am not claiming that every change is necessarily good, adding something that is very, very essential.

It is often assumed that science is changing very rapidly and that any change in science is good and always in a positive direction. But anyone who deals with science more closely knows that there are blind alleys that are encountered in science.

Contrasted to the popular notion of a great development in science is the perception that theology doesn't really develop. It's always kind of standing there or it's looking backward and not forward. In my examples of yesterday I mentioned that theology is not exactly the same after process thought. I do not necessarily mean that all of theology is, or should be, influenced by process thought. But process thought is something that has happened and cannot be ignored. Nor can we ignore existentialist philosophy, which has had its equivalent in existential theology. Paul Tillich wouldn't have written the way he did if there hadn't been an existentialist philosophy and an existentialist theology. And that couldn't have been written in the 16th or 17th century. Liberation theologies have, in the modern day, also changed the map of theology considerably. In liberation theologies I count not only Latin American and other liberation theologies, but also feminist and womanist theologies.

In Christology, you have several quests for the historical Jesus. Each of these quests has been different and all have added something. A significant change, in my estimation, has been the renaissance of Trinitarian theology that has taken place since the 1980s or so. The concept of the Trinity is not present in the Bible. It was an achievement of the early Church. It was not in dispute at all at the time of the Reformation. But it became a very bad thing to carry in one's baggage at the time of the Enlightenment, because it seemed irrational. How can something be one and at the same time three? That's irrational. So let's get rid of it. It's embarrassing to be a Christian, and to have this doctrine of the Trinity. So let's at least be silent about it. Of course I'm simplifying here. And then all of a sudden in the 1980s or so, books about Trinitarian theology began to appear. There are many reasons for that. But it is a new development in theology that has an enormous potential. Then in relation to science the concepts of interconnectedness, complexity and irrationality bring a different light. The whole image of God changes.

Those are then a few examples I would mention to illustrate development and change in theology. And that's why I think it's important that scientists and religious scholars respect each other for the complexity of the bodies of knowledge they represent.

That has often not happened, especially when it comes to religion. People have assumed that everybody can speak about religion. And maybe we must distinguish between religion and theology. Everybody should be able to speak about religion. But theology implies a critical and self-critical reflection about the content and effects of a tradition. In our case this is the Christian tradition. And that is a complicated process that needs some expertise, and knowledge, and experience. So there are clear parallels between how scientists work in natural science, and how theologians work. There are differences, but there are also analogies.

Time and Eternity

Doctoral Dissertation

Speaker 4: Your doctoral dissertation[3] deals with time and eternity and you consider questions of time in the church, natural science and theology. I would like to hear more of your focus in that work. But I would also like to hear your thoughts on the relationship of God to creation. Can you speak to the roles of immanence and transcendence? Do you see any shifts on this issue in the faiths?

Antje Jackelén: Two very small questions!

In my doctoral work I wanted to do something involving religion and science, but I didn't want to produce a major conceptual work. I wanted to bring religion and science, and in my case Christian theology and science, to the same table, allow them to speak to one question, and see what happens. I wanted to have the real symbol system of theology react with the body of scientific theories. I did not want to do what many have done and just talk about the idea of theism and ask how it relates to science. I wanted to see how these theological concepts are intertwined with each other and how they would relate to scientific methods, so I took up the question of time.

Theologically speaking, I considered the relationship between time and eternity. When I started I thought, "Well, the traditional way of doing this would be to go to philosophy and ask what has philosophy been saying about time?" And when I saw the philosophical literature I was totally discouraged, and almost thought that I would never ever get this finished. But then I encountered Paul Ricoeur's book *Time and Narrative*. His thesis is that you can only get an understanding of time if you understand time as narrated time. If that was true I did not need to go to philosophy first. What I needed was to find stories about time. I asked what is the theological story about time? And then it occurred to me—church hymns actually fit the criterion of a story because hymns express the experience of faith. Hymns are a condensed story of the Christian life repeated over and over again, and it goes on from generation to generation.

I began by reading a couple of thousand hymns in Swedish, German, and English, and asking what they tell us about time and eternity. For example, one sees how things have changed in the understanding of the relationship between time and eternity throughout the centuries. The classical hymns have a pattern that places us here in time basically getting ready for an eternity, which is the real thing. There can be bad times and there can be good times, but we know there is eternity which is our home.

If you go to modern hymns, that is hymns from the second half of the twentieth century, you often find a very different pattern. There is not even a certainty that there is a future because of such things as nuclear and environmental threats. And there is still less certainty about an eternity. It's the here and now that is important. If these hymns talk about eternity, they talk about it as something which gives value to the here and now. The here and now is no longer the prelude to eternity.

Of course I had some background in what physical theories of time were about.

Then I went to the Bible, to both the Old Testament and the New Testament, and looked at what is written there about time and eternity. There are some theologians who maintain that the Bible has a very specific linear concept of time, and that this overcomes a circular concept of time that is considered to be inferior to the notion of linear time. I found that it's not really that easy. There are both concepts of time in the Bible. And that's the way I think it should be.

From the Bible I went to the theological literature. There I found essentially three ways of talking about the relationship between time and eternity. One is the Augustinian model that says that you have eternity up there and you have time down here, and never do the two actually meet. There's an ontological and huge qualitative difference between time and eternity. Another model is the one that, for example, theologian Oscar Cullmann held. It's a model that has what I have called a quantitative difference between time and eternity. The claim is that eternity is basically like time with one exception: there's no end to it. In a sense this is reductionist. There is really nothing but infinite time. When I looked at this more closely I found that it's actually more Newtonian than it is New Testament. It's Newtonian with a kind of progress spin to it. And this idea of progress is probably less eschatological and more Enlightenment inspired. So in this model, time is not just a line, it's a line that goes slightly uphill. This is Newtonian plus Enlightenemant, but not biblical.

The third way of differentiating between time and eternity I've called the eschatological difference between time and eternity. This is the one that is the fuzziest, and most difficult to describe as a single concept. But it's definitely present, especially in the New Testament. It says that all is *already, but not yet*. For example, the Kingdom of God is already here in your midst, but not yet. You are already baptized into the death of Christ and the resurrection, but it is not yet revealed what you are going to be.

Coming to these theological concepts with some understanding of twentieth century physics, I was prepared to ask certain questions of my material. One way I found that dealing with scientific theories helped me as a theologian was in asking new questions of my theological material. These are questions I wouldn't have asked without those theories. I tried to verify that by writing a chapter about Newton and the Clarke-Leibniz debate and then moving on to the theories of relativity, quantum physics, and thermodynamics. In this I found a confirmation that this is the right direction for an adequate thinking about time and eternity. I was not trying to take something from science and apply it directly to theology. That's not the way I would like to see it work. Rather I want to see the structures and be able to see analogies in what is done in theology.

From that I moved on to the task of trying to construct or to develop a relational theology of time, built on the relationships between time and eternity.

The second part of the question was about creation and God's otherness. I plan to say something about that in the lecture today so I will postpone saying anything about it now. If it's not clear enough in the lecture we can get back to it.

Speaker 2: Isn't it possible that time is not a variable or degree of freedom in the concept of eternity? In other words time itself is something that does not exist in eternity.

Your thesis sounds very interesting. I understand it has been published in two languages, neither of which is accessible to me. Will it appear in a more user friendly language?

Antje Jackelén: Well, I won't comment on the friendliness of language here, but, yes, an English translation is planned. I can't tell you when it will appear, but the first steps have been taken.

Purgatory and Mansions

Antje Jackelén has just spoken to capitalism and the issue of purgatory. (see above under Western Christianity)

Antje Jackelén: ... He argued that before purgatory was an option, moneylenders would definitely go to hell. There was no option for them. And, therefore money lending was a very, very bad business. But purgatory has only one exit, and that is to paradise. So if the moneylender goes to purgatory, that's still bad, but eventually the moneylender will end up in paradise.

Speaker 5: I have a real problem with purgatory. I just cannot imagine leaving the earth and going to another place for a little while, then eventually to heaven.

Christ said, "In my home there are many mansions." Now what are these mansions? What for instance happens to the Muslim suicide-bombers who felt they were going to eternity with God when they crashed into the Twin Towers and the Pentagon? Is there a mansion of time? What did your thesis discover about heavenly time?

Antje Jackelén: Traditionally in the sciences we define terms and work with them. So if I wanted to work with time in the traditional fashion I would have to come up with definitions of concepts like eternity and then work with them. If they did not suffice I would have to redefine them, and so on. But I decided I wasn't going to do that. I wanted to focus on the relationships among notions rather than providing distinct definitions. What gave me courage to do this was that I had read about quantum physics. If scientists can live with uncertainty, why shouldn't I be able to test that uncertainty? So I called eternity "the other of time," because that's our perspective, and of course it's a fuzzy definition. But it does remind us that the concept is "other," and not just simply something that is like time but without end.

There is something open-ended in the concept. It helped me to see that the question of a retained identity beyond death is not necessarily the same as a retained continuity. This is what has been confused many times. Theologians talk about eternal life, and the idea that a person who dies, and who dies completely, is resurrected to eternal life. How can the person remain the same? Our usual way of thinking leads us to expect that there must be something that remains all along the timeline, because if there is an interruption there can be no continuity. (That is why the concept of the immortal soul has become popular.) Then I began thinking of eternity as the other of time. That opens up our comprehension by saying that it is not necessarily the same from God's perspective. And we may ask, "Why should retained identity be the same as continuous identity?" In my understanding of time and eternity as the other of time, this is not a necessary connection. I think that, in terms of images, people in the present have an easier way of imagining that. We can take metaphors from computers to help us. If a computer can reproduce files on demand, why shouldn't God in God's memory have all this? It seems to me that modern people can find it easier to imagine that than people a couple of hundred years ago. In a sense, technology makes it easier for us to have such thoughts.

And finally to the many mansions. That's a beautiful image if we try to argue for tolerance and diversity. The many mansions are found in the Gospel of John, which is kind of midway in the Bible between Genesis and the book of Revelation. What has intrigued me about this is that in the beginning we have the Garden, a paradise. But what do we have in the end in Revelation? It's not a return to the Garden. There's not a Garden coming down from Heaven; it's a city. And to me that's even more than many mansions. When I think of many mansions I think of just one big house. But a city implies the whole of society. And again, maybe this image has, more or less directly, inspired Christians to do science and technology. We are not called just to go back to the garden. We are called to a social life, a technology, and to an urban reality. This is also part of the image of salvation.

Christology

Speaker 6: I think the threefold distinction regarding time and eternity is very helpful. My question has to do then with the implications for Christology. The biblical notion is that in the fullness of time the appearance of the Christ occurs. How do you see that? It strikes me that there are perhaps distinctive Christologies related to those three. Does that make sense to you?

Antje Jackelén: That's a very interesting question. I have no fully developed concept here. And a quantitative model may not be very helpful here. I would rather think in the direction of developing an eschatological model with a focus on the cosmic Christ. I wonder whether it would be feasible to do that? I shall have to think more about that. But thank you for the question.

City of God

Speaker 5: I like your city model. Does your model have room for the 9/11 hijackers who gave their lives because they felt it was right? How does God, who is outside of time, see that in your city model?

Antje Jackelén: Well, I don't think I can tell you what's in the mind of God. The strength of the city model is that it suggests something that is bigger and more diverse than just one single concept of whatever eternity is. You have raised the question of what generally happens to people we perceive of as evildoers. I once heard the theologian Jürgen Moltmann speak to that image. I liked what he said. We can't tell for sure whether everybody will end up there. We don't know that for sure. We sure hope, but we don't know.

When asked the question, "What about Hitler?" he said that this process would certainly involve a transformation and it may be a radical or even a total transformation. And his way of explaining it was to say that the more evil there is the more transformation will be necessary. What if there is so much transformation that you have no chance of recognizing yourself? And I'm leaving it there. I am not simply saying, "well, that must have helped." We can draw no simple conclusions from this. But this is a way of getting at the problem and still leaving it as open as we need to.

Speaker 2: This is just a comment. I think the model of the mind of God as an infinite hard drive that presumably has never has a need for defragmentation and never crashes, would be quite fascinating. Dave Griffiths, an English Benedictine who spent most of his life in India trying to unite Christianity and Eastern religions, has stated in one of his books that the church, which is a human organization, can be compared to the walls of the city of God. He claims that in the fullness of time, the walls will disappear, faith and hope will no longer be necessary, and only love will remain. I think this is a very interesting concept.

Also in your eschatological view of Christology the concept of Alpha and Omega from Teilhard de Chardin can also be applicable.

Antje Jackelén: Thank you. To the first comment about love, I guess the only thing I can say is "Amen."

Language

Language and Mathematics

Speaker 7: This is, perhaps, testing the limitations of hermeneutics as applied to science. I can see many parallels in the way that language and thought are constructed and how that influences the way we go about the business of theology and science. How does mathematics fit into this? Do you see that as something parallel to language? In that sense, then, is mathematics also subject to self-criticism and the same suspicion that we would bring to our concepts in language, or does this really represent a separate domain?

Antje Jackelén: That's a very good question. I believe that as long as we can say "Oh this is language, these are words, and words we put together in a syntax," then we can use the methods of hermeneutics. What about if we put together numbers, or symbols in equations? I suppose one could argue that this is a case lying somewhat in between. Equations are not just numbers they are letters and symbols and they have syntax. So they are not disqualified in terms of hermeneutical analysis. But how far can you get with that? I'm going to speak to that in my third lecture. In that lecture I will discuss postmodernism. There are people who react strongly against post-modernism. They have arguments along the lines of, "Well 2+2=4 wherever you are. Don't tell me that's a construction. Don't tell me that you can deconstruct that with some kind of hermeneutical method." I'm very sympathetic with that position. Still, I am going to argue that construction is a reality. If you say that *everything* is construction, or even worse say everything is *just* construction, then you are being reductionist in the extreme. But what you can say is that everything that is comes along with construction. And there, I think, is the opening for the use of hermeneutical methods. What does it mean that everything comes along with construction? And how do you handle these constructions?

Complexity and Chaos

Speaker 8: I think that it's important to clarify the language used when speaking of chaos and complexity and their relation to the second law of thermodynamics and to entropy. There are different concepts involved in each of these. The terminology is, however, similar. Chaos is a term used to describe behavior that appears to be unpredictable, but is actually quite predictable. The problem is that where the system ends up is very sensitively affected by where it starts, like billiard balls on a table. Where the balls end up is given precisely by how we hit that first ball. But very, very slight differences give completely different results. Complex systems are also completely connected systems, but in complexity we see the emergence of something not necessarily expected. A structure emerges. We may find an understanding of this in terms of the second law of thermodynamics. Thermodynamics applies to systems consisting of vast numbers of atoms and molecules. And such systems far out of equilibrium show evidence of the emergence of structure. This is related to the production of entropy, which is a property of the second law. Complexity emerges in thermodynamic systems far from equilibrium. The concepts are linked, but different.

And what can we then say about God? If you wish to say that God is more complex than anything we can imagine you can still consider these ideas as a human picture of that. You could say that God's complex nature means that God has internal characteristics. But it also means, in this model, that God is also involved in a very deep way in all the changes of the world. This leads as well to a concept of God as changing, but yet remaining forever the same.

Antje Jackelén: Thank you for that comment. I'm aware of the fact that chaos and complexity are not the same. Maybe I should have made that clearer. But my intention was not the describing of theories. My intention was to consider order and disorder. You are correct in pointing out that there is a difference between something that is deterministic in principle and something that is regarded to be non-deterministic. My impression as a non-physicist, however, is that there is no general consensus yet on what is really what. That makes it a little difficult to make exact statements. I think this is in flux, or in progress, and there are different interpretations of it. I agree there needs to be more clarity, and perhaps there could be more clarity.

But there is more to be said. I am hesitant to jump to quick conclusions about God and complexity here for the following reason. On hearing of Einstein's theories of relativity some people tried to interpret what he was saying by claiming that everything is then relative. This is an example of the ideology building potential of scientific theories that I spoke of in my first lecture. The problem is that Einstein's theories were very distinct and precise. There was nothing relative about them in the common understanding of the word, which was often forgotten when people, inspired by physics, used the concept in various contexts. And I am critical of myself here. Am I doing the same thing when I use the concept of complexity? Am I building an ideology out of something that is a distinct scientific concept? In the case of relativity the theories were clear. But in the terms of the complexity, it's not yet very clear what this actually is. So that's why I want to be careful. But I hope to be able to develop that more.

You mentioned the changing concept of God. When I raised this issue with another audience, I remember that I got the comment, "Oh, come on, why are you so concerned about doing something to the concept of God and so afraid of talking about change in God? That is a problem that belongs to a whole different philosophy such as the concept of the unmoved mover. It is a question of Aristotelian categories. And if you leave them behind by choosing something else you shouldn't be so concerned about that." I'm not completely sure yet where I am at this point. But we need to think of the consequences in terms of God's involvement in the world and in terms of change in God. If we move in this direction we highlight something very different, and we need to ask what does that mean to our concepts of the will of God, the power of God, our concept of future, and so on. These are exciting issues in theology.

Feminism

Gender and Science

Speaker 7: This may be a trivial point, but I get to thinking. As you were speaking this morning I thought about the notion of a male scientist subduing the female matrix. That seems like a blatant example of the use of gendered terminology. How do you see this relating to the fact that in many, perhaps most, European languages nouns are gendered. *Natura* is a feminine noun. Presumably then these things are set before science comes along and utilizes them in a prejudicial way. This is now almost invisible in English, of course, but how do you see this as being related to the discussion?

Antje Jackelén: Yes and no—in regard to the relevance of grammatical gender. You can see this in the fact that science is feminine too. In the case of Bacon and many others, both nature and science were dressed in feminine clothes very deliberately. But the one got the dress of the wild woman that needs to be brought the right way, and the other got the dress of the virgin. We can of course ask why. The grammatical gender reveals something. But it doesn't determine the direction in which your understanding and work is going to go. It doesn't free us from the need of doing our hermeneutical homework. It may not be the same thing, but some people have said that we need to speak about the Holy Spirit using feminine gender, because in Hebrew it's *ruach* and that's feminine. Of course then you have the Greek *pneuma* which is neutrum and the Latin *spiritus* which is masculine as well. Elizabeth Johnson is a theologian who has pointed out that this is not the way to consider the question. There are other and better ways of accomplishing the task.

Discussions

Women in Science

Speaker 1: Is there any clear evidence of what does happen when women go into the natural sciences? Do we have any clear evidence that there are now different methods being brought to bare and different findings?

Antje Jackelén: As I said, I think it's easiest to show that it makes a difference in anthropology. There certain questions were not asked because things were being considered from the male point of view. And it was often women who realized that these questions were not being asked. For example males had looked for a confirmation that females are less sexually active, that females are more bound to infants, and that females tend to be more monogamous. It wasn't realized that often projections were being made on these questions.

Frans de Waal is one of those who, not necessarily from a gender but from a cultural perspective, has written about this. In his book *The Ape and the Sushi Master*[4] he shows how these typologies play a role in research, and may inform research in general.

An example from the other end of the spectrum took place several weeks ago when I was in a discussion with a group of students. One student claimed to have read somewhere that if the Big Bang theory had been discovered and formulated by a woman, it wouldn't have had the name Big Bang, because that's a male image. And I said, "Oh come on, how would you know?" And the particle physicist at the table said that there's basically no way that gender could play a role in particle physics.

I think you can make the case that in any area of research the metaphors and the typologies you are using play a role in how you interpret your data. And they can influence the next step you take in research. What are the next questions to ask? What choice do you make and what kind of data do you want to collect? There

I think it's relatively easy to see a possible and real influence. But that is not the same as saying that this makes a whole different kind of science.

Speaker 1: Does gender make a difference in attraction to the sciences in general? There are many places that have tried to attract more women into the fields of natural sciences. Is there something in gender differences that women are less inclined to be interested in chemistry, physics, biology, geology, and so on?

Antje Jackelén: I think there are differences that result from the pedagogy you use. It's my impression that young women who go into the sciences are often encouraged when they can see, pretty early on, what they actually can do with the science. They need to see that science is more than just learning the laws and mastering equations. We can use it to do research, and a host of other things having positive effects on the quality of life. That is a more complete or holistic picture.

In Sweden there were conscious efforts made to attract more young women to the natural science prógrams. It was often pointed out that it was necessary to have role models, to have other women in order to show the whole picture, where traditional pedagogy just got at the tiny bits and pieces.

Women and Male Images

Speaker 5: In teaching my own students about women in the sciences I have often used the example of women in astronomy and the very important contributions they have made because of their great patience. I believe that the patience and attention to detail of these women astronomers is far greater than possessed by their male colleagues.

I am reminded as well of the patient x-ray crystallography work done by Rosalind Franklin that was used by Watson and Crick, without appropriate credit I should add, in the discovery of the double helix of DNA. The story is related in the book *the Double Helix*.

Speaker 9: I just wanted to say something quickly, in response to what you said about the naming of the Big Bang. I think it is a science and religion issue in the following sense. If a woman had discovered the concept it probably still would have been called the Big Bang, because it wasn't given that name by its originators. Aleksandr Friedmann[5] was dead long before the name Big Bang was ever given to it. Fred Hoyle, who greatly opposed Friedmann's idea, probably gave the name. This has happened in religion over and over again. Their enemies at Antioch called early followers of Christ Christians. Their enemies in Germany called early followers of Luther Lutherans. It frequently happens that the naming of some concept comes from the opponents of the concept, and not from the originators.

Speaker 5: Perhaps the Big Bang should be called the Big Silence, because there was nobody there to hear it.

Speaker 4: What about the Big Birth? Would that be better?

Speaker 5: Well, you mean it's more feminine to call it the Big Birth? Some women don't cry out when they're in labor, so they're silent too.

Speaker 8: Recently a woman, considering fight or flight studies on laboratory animals, pointed out that a female laboratory animal with young, and it isn't going to fight and it's not going to flee. It's going to take care of its young. She had also observed that female animals, as well as humans, are more apt to form alliances for protection than to fight or flee. And so she reasoned that there was something wrong with the premise. Of course males also look for allies. But the point is that a woman observed a situation in laboratory animals that a man may not have observed.

Speaker 5: I would like to point out that Lynn Margulis contended that evolution was a result of symbiosis rather than survival of the fittest.

Antje Jackelén: There are two important points here that I would like to underline. The first is that we should make women more visible in the sciences. The second is that this is a continuum. The ideas are not only female or only male.

Maybe I can draw a parallel to feminist critique of theology. One part of this has been to make women in the Bible more visible. Some generations ago, many people hardly knew the name of any woman in the Bible, except Eve and Mary. Everybody who studies the Bible now gets a lot of information about women's destinies and women's lives in the Bible. I think something like this needs to happen with church history, with political and cultural history, and with the history of science. The contributions of women need to be made visible without building myths around them. It is not necessary to create macho histories. In the case of Rosalind Franklin, I have read articles that contradict the contention that she was actually abused by her colleagues. I don't know what the truth is. But I would underline the need to uncover these kinds of histories, and claim them not only for the sake of women, but for the sake of the wholeness of the history of science and the history of human kind.

Regarding the continuum, I mean that it's not necessarily women that expose what may be considered the female approach to something. Lynn Margulis was a very good example of thinking in terms of symbiosis. But Emily Martin, whom I quoted in my lecture, found a similar idea expressed by the Polish biologist Ludwik Fleck. So not only women, but also men think in these terms. It's a continuum. We should keep that in mind.

Margaret Wertheim has also contributed to this question. She asks whether or not women would have done it differently in science? She suggests that this race for the theory of everything is a typical male endeavor. What difference would it make to have this theory of everything? What difference would it make for everyday life? And if you can't show that it would make a difference, why on earth would you keep so many minds and keep so many material resources occupied with that? Would women say, well that's interesting, we should perhaps do it, but for the time being there are other questions that need more immediate attention?

Women and Competition

Speaker 4: Whether you are a man or a woman there is a tremendous amount of conformity that one must abide by in getting the Ph.D. You need to know what the basic methods are, and you need to produce something along the lines of what has been done in the past. And so I wonder if it might take more time in order to more fully assess how women would do things differently in physics or in chemistry or mathematics. These sciences need stronger female representation before we can judge whether or not there is an actual difference in approaches. Each of us is an individual and there is a continuum. But I suspect that it's partly about conformity. And it may require a fair amount of time until we see more results of role models and more freedom to help in the evolution of the field to perhaps steer it in new directions.

Speaker 10: As the discussion has gone on I have wondered about the issue of competition among women. This is a factor when we talk about the differences between men and women. I've been in several discussions about why women compete with each other and brush up against each other. I think that there's been a lot of progress made with this issue. But I think that the reason that women fight with each other or compete with each other is because they're fighting for the place of men. They are fighting to be at the top. They are fighting for the place of men in history. In order to be able to do that, you have to take on the more characteristics, attitudes, and traits that are ordinarily associated with men. One thing I'm interested in doing and working on, is dispelling some of those differences. Maybe those are innate differences between men and women, but, as you were saying, there's a continuum. The issue is not necessarily that men are this way and women are that way. If we can let men and women come with new ways to do things, as individuals, as was said here, and not have this stereotypical male or female character that might help some of this too.

Antje Jackelén: Thank you. The modern usage of gender is helpful here. This helps us see that female things are not strictly linked to women, or limited to women, and male things are not limited to men. Some say that there's no difference whatsoever in men and women doing the same kind of science. There are others who oppose this and claim that it is because you, as a woman, have been forced to adapt so much that you have forgotten your true nature, which is a problematic statement.

Whenever women, as a group, are new to a field that has traditionally been male-dominated, certain things happen. In this situation women are under pressure to be a little better than men to get the same type of recognition. So there is a competition. And in reality there are often not so many slots for women, so the competition is very, very intense. And you learn in the process not to trust each other too much.

Another thing that happens is women put themselves under continuous stress believing that we must always prove that we are at least as good as the men, which makes women sometimes more "male" than the males are.

Women also have a tendency to build empires around themselves. I think that's a natural behavior given the situation. You need to build "an empire." You need to be in control. I suppose that these are all common experiences for a new group in a field.

There is also the necessity of recognition. It's my experience that getting recognition for what you do tends to be different for men than for women. At the same time, having said this about competition and the pitting of women against each other, we also have wonderful examples of how women just do something other than competing. This includes building social structures and developing cooperation. There is much to gain from the advantages cooperative projects have over and against competitive projects.

Postmodernism

Defined

Speaker 11: Can postmodern be defined?

Antje Jackelén: I would say it's difficult to give a very simple and precise definition. Of course definitions might vary from person to person. For me a definition of postmodernism would involve the identification of certain phenomena and certain thoughts that appear over and over again. The reason why I chose to talk about nature for quite a while in the beginning (of the lecture) was not to say, "Oh, there's nothing new. It's already there." Rather I wanted to say, "it's not radically new. It has roots going back in time. It's both something new and also thoughts that you can find elsewhere."

Speaker 2: Can you give a date at which you would say postmodern ideas became important?

Antje Jackelén: I think the term postmodern was used as early as 1917. But it was definitely not a well-known term at that time. We have come to know it in architecture and it has a link to aesthetics. It also has links to narratives and to story. But I am also aware that critics have said, "Oh, postmodernists are these people who say sentences that nobody understands and if they get caught at it they just recite a poem."

Speaker 2: The reason I asked the question about dates is that modernism became a bad word with the Catholic Church between 1910-1915. The condemnation of modernism by Pius X was, of course, repealed with Vatican II in the 1964-65. But it seems to me that post modernism would be represented, at least in the Catholic mind, by what happened since 1965.

Antje Jackelén: Maybe you could say that.

Speaker 9: I want to put in a word for sensitivity in the use of terminology here. In philosophy, theology, or the history of ideas, the term modern refers to the ideas of the Enlightenment. The period encompasses the ides of Francis Bacon up through the point at which postmodern enters. But in science in general, and in physics in particular, the term modern doesn't mean that at all. In the language of the physicist classical physics begins with Newtonian physics (1687). Modern physics begins with the developments of relativity and quantum physics in the twentieth century. The roots are earlier, of course, in the latter part of the nineteenth century.

Antje correctly says that this is postmodern in spirit. However, the basis of the quantum theory is a lot more definite than most things about postmodernism that you would hear from philosophers, literary critics etc. Quantum theory partakes a great deal of the same world-view as postmodernism as opposed to classical physics which is enlightenment and modernism, although most physicists prefer not to lump themselves in the same category as some postmodern philosophers. I think the Catholic Church was arguing against the Enlightenment.

Truth and Judgment

Speaker 6: I'd like to go back to this notion of the noble competition of the best candidates for the truth. I am reminded that everything is not up for grabs. In fact there are some claims that have more validity based on some criteria in postmodern thought. Are there criteria by which competing interpretations can be evaluated? Is there a set of rules by which such a competition is judged or is the whole notion of rules even problematic?

While I hold the microphone I also have a second question as well. Do religion and science, broadly speaking, have competing criteria for making such kinds of judgments?

Antje Jackelén: In one sense you can probably say that postmodernism also complicates the notion of rules. It is not that there are no rules. But postmodernism asks questions like, who makes the rules and for whom. And who has the defining power of making the rules, and so on. So it reveals to me, in a stronger sense, the role of consensus in rules. Who has decided that a consensus exists regarding these rules to which we are adhering? As long as you are as aware as possible of the rules to which we are adhering, and if you can stick to the rules, then that's how it works. So it's not about negating the value or even the function or necessity of rules. Of course this is a very constructive and benevolent reading of postmodernism. Postmodernism then sharpens our sensitivity to the fact that rules are not just dumped on us from somewhere else. There is a lot of construction involved there.

Are there competing rules in religion and science? This reminds me of the notion of non-overlapping magisteria (S. J. Gould) or strongly overlapping magisteria. There are a lot of things that overlap. Otherwise we wouldn't have been able to carry on a dialog more or less successfully for more than a couple of years. So that already tells me that we have a lot of rules that actually strongly overlap.

Discussions 115

Present and Future

Speaker 11: Do you see the discussion of postmodernity declining now? Five or ten years ago it seems that it was all I heard in the field of philosophy and religion. There were certain people who identified with the movement claiming to be postmodern. I am sure there is always something like that. Does this sort of differentiation still exist? I'm ready to concede that it's not a fad, but I no longer hear much about it. It is something with validity and for which you can find roots in ancient Greece. But I do identify with the need to take more care of defining the terms and making a commitment to something that is somewhat solid and in which is respectful of tradition.

Antje Jackelén: I hear the word postmodern used more in a popular sense and it could mean almost anything. Usually when people say, "Oh you know in postmodern times, when we are confronted with pluralism and it's hard to make really absolute and binding statements, you have to cope with pretty much everything." That is of course a popular conception and it can essentially mean anything you choose.

Speaking about postmodernism in a broad cultural sense I would say one of the most significant marks of a postmodern attitude toward life is what sociologist Zygmunt Bauman, who is Polish and working in Britain, has expressed. He says we are no longer *pilgrims*, but we are *nomads*. What he means is that in the postmodern time you don't believe in long-term projects anymore. That is one of the most dramatic features postmodernism. If you don't believe in long term projects, and if you think in the terms of the individual person, nothing you do is for life. You don't choose an occupation for life. You don't have a job for life. You don't have a partner for life. You don't have a place where you live for life. You don't have an identity for life anymore. Everything is just in flux and changing.

That of course has serious consequences. How can you conceive of your own life work and how can you conceive of a project for your society? It would be difficult to base an ecological ethics on such a concept. Why would we care what the world looks like for our grandchildren if we are postmodern in that sense? It would be hard to argue for the concept of long-term sustainability if we were really 100% postmodern in this sense. Such concerns would simply be beyond our horizon.

At the same time I think that another feature of postmoderninsm, the tension between sameness and otherness, will stay with us for a while. I see that as the struggle we have in our culture. We want the otherness, we want the tolerance, we want the diversity, but we can't just have only diversity and nothing else. We need to have this sense of a base, of being grounded somewhere. We want to affirm diversity as much as possible, but still not lose a connection to the center or whatever image we may use for that.

Hermeneutics

Speaker 2: Hermeneutics really teaches us to not only look at the text but behind the text as well as in front of the text. And it is interesting to look at not only what Nietzsche said but also who he was and how he got there. A great modern Swiss psychoanalyst, Alice Miller, has written a very interesting book entitled *The Untouched Key* in which she examines the influence that the very early environment up to the age of 3 or 4 has upon the future of an individual. She considered several examples of notable people such as, for example, Pablo Picasso, Friedrich Nietzsche and also Adolf

Hitler. She was able to identify a source for many of Nietzsche's ideas in the very difficult family environment that he had as a child. She also noted the influence that Nietzsche had on other people such as Hitler and his philosophy. In the positive sense you might say that Nietzsche had a reasonable influence upon another giant of the German school, namely Richard Strauss. In any event it is interesting to notice how this influence was important in shaping Nietzsche's life and philosophy.

Antje Jackelén: Of course you can always debate how much it may have mattered that he grew up in this pastor's house, with a father who fell ill and died when he was five, and having only females around him, and all of that. I wouldn't say, however, that you necessarily have a causal relationship between the outcome of his philosophy and that difficult early childhood. And that is probably not what you mean. Certainly in Nietzsche's case there are the problems behind the scenes. I agree with you that his life story has an impact on his philosophy. Such things often have a contradictory influence. His affirmation of life is in contrast to his own life, which was restricted in many ways. And he tells us that he suffered from a lot of things. So it seems that he never really could have had this hedonistic enjoyment of life. But saying that this difficult life is the only source would be to do too much. A lot of other interesting situations existed. He came across Schopenhauer's work and that obviously influenced him. He ran into Schopenhauer's work in a bookstore, was fascinated by it and dealt with it in various ways throughout his active period.

Speaker 5: Can you tell everybody how he died? I thought it was so interesting.

Antje Jackelén: The last days of Nietzsche are interesting in light of his fierce critique of Christianity. Nietzsche held that Christianity had forced upon us a slave mentality based on resentment and negative feelings. His idea of the *Übermensch* was a free spirit not subject to a slave mentality. Nietzsche believed that the slave mentality was kept in place not only by resentment, but also by compassion. He attacked compassion over and over again.

In the end compassion is the last sin that Zarathustra has to overcome. And why is compassion a sin? Compassion is a sin because it forces weakness upon us. Compassion encourages weakness. If I have compassion for you I am saying that you are weak and that I affirm your weakness. And in my affirmation of weakness in you I accept weakness in myself. Weakness encourages the slave mentality. And for that reason Nietzsche was opposed to compassion.

The interesting incident happens toward the end of his life, at the beginning of his insanity. In Turin, Italy, in January of 1889, he saw a cabman beating a horse. He was overcome with compassion for the horse, stepped forward, fell into tears, and hugged the horse. And he never became sane again. The irony is that he who claimed that compassion was the last sin of Christianity, in his final act before falling ill (he died in 1900) showed compassion for a horse that was beaten.

I should also say something about dance. Dance is a very essential metaphor that Nietzsche uses over and over again. And I have tried to understand why. It doesn't seem to me that he was a wonderful dancer. That is not the reason. I think the reason is that his philosophy of life says that life is to be lived in its fullest. That means to experience the ecstasy as well as the agony of life. Nietzsche did not settle for a life that is only heavy. He wanted life that has the fullness of beauty, the dance, as well. I think this is where the dance metaphor comes from. In the dance one is extended. In the dance one is in motion and not static. In the dance one affirms life in its fullest. That's at least part of it.

Reflecting on what has been said here, I think one can make a general—but not necessarily exact—statement about a difference between hermeneutics, in the more sober sense, and postmodernism. Hermeneutics often used to say that what is behind and what is in front of the text are both important. Postmodernism seems to abandon more and more what is behind the text and focus almost exclusively on what is in front of the text.

Eastern Orthodoxy

Speaker 5: You were saying religious communities have a duty to look into ways in which we can dialogue on science and religion and you mentioned the Eastern Orthodox as being very important. Would you amplify on that please?

Antje Jackelén: For the moment let me speak only about the Christian family without considering other religions. I would say that within the larger family of Christian churches the Orthodox Churches have been the least represented in dialogue for various reasons.

One reason, of course, is that Orthodox Churches have had problems with ecumenism. In my experience it is often better, or at least easier, to get people to talk science and religion than to get them to talk about their different belief traditions. They might not be allowed to talk about their faith traditions or they might not want to talk about them. They may never come to any consensus regarding these traditions. But there may be consensus about science, technology, and ethics, and so on.

Also when I raised the concept of wisdom I did so knowing

that in Eastern Orthodox theology the concept of wisdom is a very central one. I am especially thinking of Sergii Bulgakov, a Russian theologian who like many other Russian theologians of the twentieth century was in exile in Paris. He developed the concept that is called Sophiology from Sophia, Wisdom.[6] At least partially based on this he was declared to be a heretic. He wrote another book, in order to become more accepted, but that is not so interesting. The interesting point is that wisdom is essential to the orthodox faith position, but it is also controversial. That is one of the reasons I think wisdom is a good topic for consideration. Wisdom is also something that comes up in Nietzsche—transcending, in a sense, the critique he has of both science and Christianity. It is a concept that is brought up as well by ecologists. They insist that if we are going to think in terms of sustainability and wholeness of the earth, then we must have a really inclusive concept on which to base this and that is going to be wisdom. Since the concept of wisdom emerges from many corners, I have the impression that it might be good to have a discussion about it.

Speaker 5: The Eastern Orthodox rites in the Catholic Church, as well, are very much attuned to the transcendence of God rather than the immanence. Is that what you mean by transcendence versus immanence?

Antje Jackelén: It's part of the picture. And it's part of the reason that, historically speaking, there is a difference in the connection between the priests in the Christian churches (of the East and the West) and the development of science. Many of the pioneers of classical science (in the West) were priests. You don't have that connection in the Eastern Orthodox tradition. Part of the reason for this is certainly the difference in eschatology and the difference in Christology between the churches. The western tradition focuses more on the crucified Christ and on following Christ as the goal of the disciples of Christ. Followers of Christ heal the sick and try to make the world a better place. The eastern tradition focuses more on the resurrected Christ. In a sense this is a focus on the transcendence of God as the means by which the world is transformed into the reign of God.

Speaker 5: I agree that science should more naturally result from an immanent concept of God. In light of this, how does the Eastern Orthodox Church relate to science?

Antje Jackelén: It is almost impossible to give a general answer to this, but I can at least refer to a book that is about to come out by Alexei Nesteruk, who is a physicist working in England, and Russian by birth. The title of the book is *Light from the East*.[7] I recommend it although I don't know what is in it. I haven't read it yet because it hasn't appeared. I think it is interesting, however, that we finally have a book on religion and science that focuses on contributions from the Eastern Orthodox Churches.

Epistemology and Brain Science

Speaker 6: It seems to me that one of the issues postmodernism raises in the discussion is that of epistemology. This, in turn, is related to the way in which the brain understands the world. In the brain sciences the idea of a meaning-making brain is discussed. That is the brain imposes structure and order on an otherwise unknowable world. Some of these thoughts emerge out of the studies of consciousness. It is this basic interpretive function of the brain that a lot of people see as supportive of a postmodern understanding of epistemology. There is a dilemma, however. If you are a thoroughgoing postmodernist I assume you also have to acknowledge the tentativeness of those interpretations of the brain.

That is, the brain is actually interpreting itself as well. And the question of where to plant oneself can become quite cyclic. I would be interested to know if anything here connects with your understanding of postmodernism.

Antje Jackelén: Well if in the sense that postmodernism tends to be a very flexible phenomenon this certainly is. But I don't know whether I can say something very intelligent about this because I simply don't know enough about neuroscience yet. I know that there are people with knowledge in brain science here. Maybe someone else would like to speak to this.

Speaker 8: What we know about memory supports this. Working memory can only bring maybe four things to the table at a time and have, perhaps, seven things actively in play. And those things come from different directions. For example, Antonio Damasio has pointed out the importance of emotion in what may be called rational thought. It is emotion that allows us to make rational decisions.

What we hear from others is also important for the working consciousness. The brain is not completely determined genetically. The human genome, with 30,000 genes simply does not contain enough information to determine the neurons and the neuron connections in the human brain.[8] The interactions with the environment and particularly other people are crucial in constructing the connections in the human brain. So this, I think, is a physical substrate to the fact that our understandings of reality have to be.

Speaker 12: Whenever we speak of a scientific understanding we should realize that the brain is consciously thinking about the brain. This is the point that was raised. Modern experimental, and consequently theoretical, science deals with a universe that is separate from the scientist. For example, all of our understanding of large complex systems is based on a highly developed statistical mechanics and an explicit assumption that certain measurements can be made. I am not referring here to quantum limitations. The issue is our understanding of the concept of measurement itself. As long as the system being studied can be separated from the observer we know what this is. But when we consider the brain we must acknowledge that the system is the observer. This is new ground in theoretical physics.

We almost easily speak of the brain as if we were separate from it. I suspect that this attitude will need to change scientifically before we can make progress in much of this.

Antje Jackelén: Thank you.

Perhaps we should not focus on autopoietic (from Greek: autos/self + poiein/make) systems alone. Just the notion of *auto*poietic systems is a reflection of the individual patterns we put on what we see, whereas a more consciously postmodern approach would say, "Wait a minute, is it at all possible that something is really *autos*? Should we rather be looking at things as being developed from many sources?" Then maybe we should speak of communio-poetic systems instead (although this word is a hybrid of Latin and Greek). At this point, I have no empirical evidence for such a communio-poietic interpretation of systems. It is just a question that came to me from the thoughts I was having. This is something of a demonstration of how the hermeneutical process works and the way in which the questions we ask of material can actually inform what kind of results we get. We often get what we are looking for.

Theologians

Speaker 1: One footnote about the dance. Although all scientists may not dance well, most have a deep appreciation for aesthetic beauty. Scientists claim that if it is not beautiful it cannot be truth. The scientists that I know at Goshen College certainly have an appreciation for aesthetic beauty.

The question I have for you, Professor Jackelén, is how does Barth fit into this? Are there theologians who are good examples of postmodernism? Particularly, what can be said about Karl Barth?

Antje Jackelén: Well, I think it is problematic to consider Karl Barth to be a postmodernist. This is put in focus if we ask why Barth was not interested in the dialogue between science and religion. One of the reasons, of course, was this division between God and the "non-God." This is what Dietrich Bonhoeffer described critiqued as revelation positivism. In this sense Barth is too positivist to become postmodern. Now, as is the case with all truly great writers, you might find something in Barth that you could use to argue that he is postmodern. For example, you could draw on Barth's thoughts on God's otherness and link it to Lévinas, Derrida and Marion. But the general impression would probably be that he doesn't fit.

There are among modern theologians many that have in one way or another been influenced or impressed by postmodernism. I recently listened to the public defense of a dissertation entitled "The Return of God" by Jayne Svenungsson, a young Swedish theologian. She draws from Nietzsche and then goes on through the French postmodernists Derrida, Deleuze, Lévinas and Marion to show how they deal with the question of God. One of the things she pointed out was that whatever was meant in Nietzsche by the death of God was, in a sense, a presupposition for the return of

God in postmodernism. Now it is interesting to note that when postmodernists bring God to the table they often do so using Augustine, especially his *Confessions*. Derrida for example has a piece with the title *Circonfession* which is a play of words on the Augustinian Confessions. Yet, postmodern philosophers can be criticized for not paying enough attention to theology. They do not always realize that many of the things they are doing now have already been done in theology. Not the least of these is the "God is dead" theology of the 1960s. This sort of immanentist theology has already been done. And we are far beyond that. It seems that some early postmodern philosophy in its critique of metaphysical transcendence repeated that.

On similar grounds I criticized some of the scientists who write in science and religion. Often they write as though theology is the same today as in the time of Galileo. All too often progress in theology is being neglected. Philosophers can obviously make the same mistake. The belief is that a kind of theistic structure is all you need to know when you talk about God. But what needs to happen is engagement with distinct theological ideas and concepts.

Today there are a number of people who have constructively engaged postmodern thinking in their theologies.

Speaker 1: The reason I mentioned Barth is that he abandons the idea that there are some absolute truths. There is the inherent appeal of Christ as the incarnation of God that you must accept in order to see the validity of it. You can't prove that to someone outside of the tradition.

Antje Jackelén: Yes, that would be at least an attempt to see some closeness. I would need to think more about it.

Speaker 9: With regard to immanence and transcendence in the Eastern Orthodox tradition, I think that one needs to realize that, perhaps even more so than in the Roman Catholic Church, Eastern Orthodox is centered around the liturgy. The details are different here and there. But in both the mass and the Eastern Orthodox liturgy, which would include a lot of Eastern Rite Catholics, there are really two high points to the liturgy. One high point, maybe the highest, is the actual communion, which is the immanence of Christ. This is present in Eastern Orthodoxy just as it is in Catholicism. Although there is a lot of transcendence in Eastern Orthodoxy, I think there is a great mystical feeling of immanence which is at the highest point of the liturgy. There is another high point in both the mass and the eastern liturgy and that is when the gospel is read. Just before the gospel is read in the Eastern Orthodox Church the deacon cries "Wisdom!"

Speaker 5: Teilhard de Chardin mentioned Nietzsche's "you shall not only reproduce yourself, but produce upward." And that is exactly how he felt. He was a pilgrim of the future and he always wanted to move upward toward point Omega.

Antje Jackelén: Thank you. These are both good points.

Index

A
aesthetic beauty, 124
Agential realism, 46
Albright, John, 51
Alexandria, 16
American Indians, 42
anamnesis, 62
anthropocentrism, 53
anthropology, 44, 74
Antioch, 16
Apollo and Dionysus, 63
Aquinas, 52
Aristotle, 18, 35
artificial intelligence, 74
Augustine, 18, 125
autopoietic systems, 51, 68, 123

B
Bacon, Francis, 35, 40, 64, 104
Barad, Karen, 46
Barrow, John, 40
Barth, Karl, 18, 124
Bauman, Zygmunt, 115
Big Bang, 105
Blosser, Don, 11
Boccaccio, 88
Bohr, Niels, 22, 46, 69
Bonhoeffer, Dietrich, 124
Born, Max, 67

Brock, Rita Nakashima, 33
Bulgakov, Sergii, 73, 120
Bultmann, Rudolf, 18

C
capitalism, 88
Caputo, John, 65, 70
chance and determinism, 49
chaos, 101
Chaos theory, 49
Charybdis, 64, 70
Christian life, 93
Christian tradition, 85
Christology, 90, 98, 120
Clarke, Samuel, 25, 94
classical hymns, 93
classical physics, 113
Clement of Alexandria, 16
cloning, 74
communio-poietic, 123
complementarity, 25, 31, 49
complex systems, 50, 123
complexification, 49
complexity, 48, 101
consciousness, 121
Copenhagen, 24
Cosmic Christ, 98
Cosmos and Creation, 7
creation theology, 86

D

Damasio, Antonio, 122
Dante, 88
Darwin, Charles, 32
Davies, Paul, 27
de Chardin, Teilhard, 99, 126
de Waal, Frans, 45, 105
Deane-Drummond, Celia, 73
Deleuze, Gilles, 124
Deloria, Vine, 41
Derrida, Jacques, 55, 65, 124
Descartes, René, 65
dialog, 86
Dilthey, Wilhelm, 19
Dionysian spirit, 57
disciples of Christ, 121

E

Easter, 86
Eastern Orthodox, 73, 119
Eastern Orthodox liturgy, 126
Eastern Orthodox rites, 120
Eastern Orthodoxy, 87
Eastern Rite Catholics, 126
Einstein, Albert, 23, 26, 32, 102
emotion, 122
Enlightenment, 54, 65, 113
entropy, 101
entropy production, 101
epistemic community, 72
epistemology, 121
eschatology, 87, 120
eternal life, 96
eternity, 92, 94
eu-tonos, 75
everything, theory of, 40
existentialism, 58

F

Faraday, Michael, 75
Feynman, Richard, 37
Fleck, Ludwik, 45, 109
Fleming, Alexander, 30
Florensky, Pavel, 73
Frayn, Michael, 24
Friedmann, Aleksandr, 107

G

Gadamer, Hans-Georg, 19
Gaia, 40
Galileo, 32
Genesis, 49, 97
Gibb, Sir Hamilton, 85
God and complexity, 48, 53
God and creation, 52
God and freedom, 52
God and order, 48
God and simplicity, 52
God and transformative power, 53
God as complex, 101
God created, 51
God with creation, 52
God, death of, 55, 124
God, image of, 87
God's memory, 97
great apes, 45
Gregersen, Niels Henrik, 51
Griffiths, Dave, 99

H

Haraway, Donna, 47
Harding, Sandra, 47
Hawking, Stephen, 27, 32
heaven, 96
Heidegger, Martin, 19
Heisenberg, Werner, 22
hell, 89
heresies, 16
hermeneutics, 16
Hexapla, 16
Holmes, Barbara Ann, 42
Holy Spirit, 104
Howell, Nancy, 44, 47
Hoyle, Fred, 107
Hrdy, Sarah Blaffer, 45
human genome, 122
Human Genome Project, 68
Huygens, Christiaan, 32
hymns, 93

I

immanence, 92
immanentism, 71
immanentist, 125

Index

instrumentalization, 74
International Society for Science and Religion, 41
intersubjectivity, 56
Islam, 85

J

Jeanrond, Werner, 18
Jesus, historical, 32
Johnson, Elizabeth, 49, 73, 104
joyful wisdom, 60
Just, E. E., 44

K

Kant, Immanuel, 21
Keller, Evelyn Fox, 47
kenosis, 74
killer T cells, 45
Kingdom of God, 94
Kuhn, Thomas, 27

L

Lakatos, Imre, 29
Latour, Bruno, 33
Laudan, Larry, 29
Leibniz, Wilhelm Gottfried, 25, 94
Lessing, Gotthold Ephraim, 66
Lévinas, Emanuel, 55, 65, 71, 124
liberation theologies, 48, 90
Lind, Millard, 11
Loyola College in Maryland, 7
Lutherans, 107
Lyotard, Jean-François, 66

M

mansion of time, 95
Margulis, Lynn, 108
Marion, Jean-Luc, 55, 124
Martin, Emily, 44, 109
mathematics, 100
Mc Fague, Sallie, 47
measurement, 123
memory, 122
Merchant, Carolyn, 39
Midgley, Mary, 40
Miller, Alice, 116
mimesis, 62

modern hymns, 93
modern physics, 113
Moltmann, Jürgen, 73, 98
monasteries, 87
Moore, James F., 27
Morgan, T. H., 44
Muhammad, 85
Mujerista, 47
multifaith. religious communities, 73
Murphy, Nancey, 7
Muslim culture, 86
Muslim scholars, 86

N

narrated time, 92
Natura, 104
Newton, Isaac, 25, 32, 52, 94
Nietzsche, Friedrich, 14, 24, 54
Nietzsche and science, 56
Nietzsche, childhood, 117
Nietzsche, dance, 118
Nietzschean dancer, 63
Nietzsche's death of God, 59
Noble, David, 41
nomads, 115

O

observer, 123
order and disorder, 50
Origen, 16

P

paradigm, 27
paradise, 89
Pederson, Ann, 47
perspectivism, 54
Peters, Karl, 61
Petrarch, 88
Pius X, 112
Platonism, 61
poiesis, 62
positivism, 58
postfoundationalist, 29
postmodern philosophy, 54
primatology, 46
progress, 89
purgatory, 88, 95

Q
quantum physics, 94

R
Ramadan, 86
Reformation Churches, 87
relativity, 94
Revelation, 97
revelation positivism, 124
Ricoeur, Paul, 20, 92
Roman Catholicism, 87
Röntgen, Wilhelm Conrad, 30
Royal Society, 37
Ruach, 104
rules, 114
Russian Orthodoxy, 87

S
salvation, 97
salvation history, 85
Schiebinger, Londa, 39
Schleiermacher, Friedrich, 18
Schopenhauer, Arthur, 117
scientific community, 28
Scylla, 64, 70
second law of thermodynamics, 49, 101
semper reformanda, 21
serendipity, 30
Shiva, Vandana, 39, 47
sophiology, 73, 120
Spain, 86
spirituality, 87
spiritus pneuma, 104
statistical mechanics, 123
stem cell research, 74
Stengers, Isabelle, 31
Stenmark, Lisa, 47
suicide-bombers, 96
symbol system, 92
syntax, 100

T
Theodore of Mopsuestia, 17
theological hermeneutics, 15
theosis, 74
thermodynamics, 95
Thomas Aquinas, 52
Tillich, Paul, 90
time, 92
time in the Bible, 93
time without end, 94
time, Augustinian model, 94
Tipler, Frank, 27
transcendence, 92
transformation, 99
Traweek, Sharon, 42
Trinitarian, 90
Trinitarian God, 52
Trinitarian theology, 49
Trinity, 90
Trinity and Newton, 26
truth, 113
Tuana, Nancy, 42
twin towers, 96

U
Übermensch, 56, 118
uncertainty, 96

V
Vatican II, 112
Vattimo, Gianni, 65

W
Waddington, C. H., 44
Watt, William Montgomery, 85
Weinberg, Stephen, 27
Wertheim, Margaret, 40, 109
wisdom, 120, 126
Wittgenstein, Ludwig, 51

Z
Zarathustra, 57, 60, 118

Notes

Editor's Preface

1   Nancey Murphy and George F. R. Ellis, *On the Moral Nature of the Universe*, (Kitchener: Pandora Press, 2003).

Lectures: The Challenge of Hermeneutics

1   Friedrich Nietzsche, "Jenseits von Gut und Böse, Vorspiel einer Philosophie der Zukunft," in *Sämtliche Werke, Kritische Studienausgabe, Band 5*, eds. Giorgio Colli and Mazzino Montinari (München and Berlin/New York: Deutscher Taschenbuch Verlag and Walter de Gruyter, 1980), 53.
2   John Caputo, *More Radical Hermeneutics* (Bloomington and Indianapolis: Indiana University Press, 2000), 156.
3   Werner Jeanrond, *Theological Hermeneutics: Development and Significance* (London: SCM Press, 1994), 20.
4   Origenes, *Vier Bücher von den Prinzipien*, edited, translated, with critical notes by Herwig Görgemanns and Heinrich Karpp, 3rd ed. (Darmstadt: Wissenschaftliche Buchgesellschaft, 1992).
5   The content of Book IV of *On First Principles* is structured as follows: IV 1: That the Scriptures are Divinely Inspired; IV 2: That Many by Not Understanding the Scriptures Spiritually and by Badly Understanding Them Fall into Heresies; IV 3: Examples from the Scriptures of How Scripture Should Be Understood, (starting out with pointing out the unreasonableness of taking Gen. 1, 5-13,

Gen. 2, 8f and others literally); IV 4: A Summary Concerning the Father, the Son, and the Holy Spirit and Other Matters Previously Discussed.

6 Gerhard Ebeling, "Hermeneutik," in *Religion in Geschichte und Gegenwart*, 3rd ed., vol. 3 (Tübingen: Mohr [Siebeck], 1959), 247: "die erste systematische Erörterung des h[ermeneutisch]en Problems."

7 Heinrich Karpp, "Einführung (I-V)," in Origenes, *Prinzipien*, 12, describes Origen's goal and method in theological work as an attempt and way, "[v]on dem Fundament des kirchlichen Glaubens durch biblische Exegese und Vernunftüberlegung zu einer 'divina scientia' emporzusteigen" (to ascend from the foundation of ecclesial faith via biblical exegesis and rational deliberations toward a 'divine knowledge'). See also Lothar Lies, *Origenes' "Peri Archon": Eine undogmatische Dogmatik* (Darmstadt: Wissenschaftliche Buchgesellschaft, 1992), 29-44, or Henri de Lubac, *Histoire et esprit: l'Intelligence de l'Écriture d'après Origène* (Paris: Aubier, 1950).

8 Origen, *An Exhortation to Martyrdom, Prayer and Selected Works*, trans. Rowan A. Greer, (New York: Paulist Press, 1979), 31.

9 Origenes, *Prinzipien*, IV 3, 15.

10 Ibid., IV 2, 2.

11 E.g. IV 4, 14 "sensum nostrum regulae pietatis aptare": "But in all these speculations let our understanding have sufficient coherence with the rule of piety."

12 Rowan Greer, "Introduction," in Origen, *Exhortation*, 32.

13 Jeanrond, *Theological Hermeneutics*, 21.

14 His five books "Contra allegoricos" have been lost according to Ebeling, "Hermeneutik," 248.

15 Jeanrond, *Theological Hermeneutics*, 21.

16 Ibid., 22.

17 Ibid., 42.

18 Ibid., 43.

19 Ibid., 22ff.

20 Hans-Georg Gadamer, *Truth and Method*, trans. Joel Weinsheimer and Donald G. Marshall, 2nd revised ed., (New York: Continuum, 1995).

21 Cf. Gadamer, *Truth and Method*, 1995, and Georgia Warnke, *Gadamer: Hermeneutics, Tradition and Reason*, (Stanford: Stanford University Press, 1987).

22 Paul Ricoeur, *Interpretation Theory: Discourse and the Surplus of Meaning* (Fort Worth: Texas Christian University Press, 1976), 94, quoted in Jeanrond, *Theological Hermeneutics*, 73.

23 "Interpretation Matters: Science and Religion at the Crossroads," a conference hosted by the Metanexus Institute for Science and Religion at Haverford College, Haverford, Pennsylvania, June 15-20, 2002.

24 Werner Heisenberg, *Physics and Beyond: Encounters and Conversations*, trans. Arnold J. Pomerans (New York: Harper & Row, 1971), 138.

25 Heisenberg, *Physics and Beyond*, 134. At this point they differ diametrically from the philosophy of the Royal Society as put forward in Thomas Sprat,

History of the Royal Society, edited by Jackson I. Cope and Harold Whitmore Jones (St. Louis: Washington University Press, 1958), 327. Sprat states that a lot of words and metaphors will be eliminated without any loss, only to use strong metaphors in his next sentence (last sentence of this quote): "What can we lose, but only some few *definitions*, and idle *questions*, and empty *disputations*? Of which I may say as one did of *Metaphors, Poterimus vivere sine illis* [we will be able to live without them]. Perhaps there will be no more use of Twenty, or Thirty obscure Terms, such as *Matter*, and *Form, Privation, Entelichia*, and the like. But to supply their want, and [sic] infinit [sic] variety of *Inventions, Motions*, and *Operations*, will succeed in the place of words. The Beautiful Bosom of *Nature* will be Expos'd to our view: we shall enter into its *Garden*, and tast [sic] of its *Fruits*, and satisfy our selves with its *plenty*."

26 Heisenberg, *Physics and Beyond*, 135.
27 Heisenberg, *Physics and Beyond*, 137
28 Werner Heisenberg, "Sprache und Wirklichkeit in der modernen Physik," in *Gesammelte Werke/Collected Works. Abteilung C: Allgemeinverständliche Schriften. Philosophical and Popular Writings, II. Physik und Erkenntnis 1956-1968*, eds. W. Blum, H.-P. Dürr and H. Rechenberg (München and Zürich: Piper, 1984), 288-301.
29 Albrecht Fölsing, *Albert Einstein: Eine Biographie*, 3rd ed. (Frankfurt/Main: Suhrkamp, 1994), 579. Cf. also Antje Jackelén, *Zeit und Ewigkeit: Die Frage der Zeit in Kirche, Naturwissenschaft und Theologie* (Neukirchen-Vluyn: Neukirchener, 2002), 214-220.
30 Cf. Evelyn Fox Keller, *Secrets of Life, Secrets of Death: Essays on Language, Gender and Science* (New York and London: Routledge, 1992).
31 Friedrich Nietzsche, *The Gay Science*, trans. Josefine Nauckhoff, ed. Bernard Williams (Cambridge: Cambridge University Press, 2001), 55.
32 Bernhard Dick, "Das Verhältnis von Glaube und Naturwissenschaft aus der Sicht eines Laien," in *Glaube und Denken: Jahrbuch der Karl-Heim-Gesellschaft*, 14. Jahrgang, ed. Hans Schwarz (Frankfurt, et al.: Peter Lang, 2001), 150.
33 H.G. Alexander, ed., *The Leibniz-Clarke Correspondence* (Manchester: Manchester University Press, 1956).
34 Michel John Petry, "Newton, Isaac (1643-1727)" in *Theologische Realenzyklopädie*, vol. 24 (New York and Berlin: Walter de Gruyter, 1994), 427, and Richard S. Westfall, *Never at Rest: A Biography of Isaac Newton* (Cambridge: Cambridge University Press, 1980), 311ff.
35 Although both Leibniz and Newton invented the calculus, they used different notations, and Newton was more preoccupied with the initial conditions than Leibniz was.
36 Jackelén, *Zeit und Ewigkeit*, 206ff.
37 James F. Moore, "Cosmology and Theology: The Reemergence of Patriarchy," *Zygon: Journal of Religion and Science* 30.4 (1990): 621.
38 Thomas Kuhn, *The Structure of Scientific Revolutions*, 2nd enl. ed. (Chicago: University of Chicago Press, 1970).

39 Ibid., 42.
40 Ibid., 172.
41 J. Wentzel van Huyssteen, *The Shaping of Rationality: Toward Interdisciplinarity in Theology and Science* (Grand Rapids: Eerdmans, 1999).
42 According to Thomas Lerner, "Det gäller att bejaka slumpen," *Dagens Nyheter* Jan 30, 2003, the word "serendipity" was created by Horace Walpole in 1754 after he had read 'an extremely simple fairy tale with the name *Three princes from Serendip* (now Sri Lanka); wherever they came through, by chance and acumen, they made discoveries of things they were not out for.'
43 Margaret Wertheim, *Pythagoras' Trousers: God, Physics, and the Gender Wars* (New York: W.W. Norton, 1997), 161ff.
44 See, for example, James McAllister, *Beauty and Revolution in Science* (Ithaca and London: Cornell University Press, 1999).
45 Isabelle Stengers, *D'une science à l'autre: Des concepts nomades* (Paris: Seuil, 1987).
46 Bruno Latour, "Give Me a Laboratory and I Will Raise the World," in *The Science Studies Reader*, ed. Mario Biagioli (New York and London: Routledge, 1999), 273. Originally published in Karen Knorr-Cetina and Michael Mulkay, eds., *Science Observed* (London: Sage, 1983 [abridged, 1998]), 141-170.
47 In addition, the question of what should be defined as a benefit proves to be rather intricate. What are the values behind the definition of what counts as a benefit? Speaking in terms of anthropology, is longevity a universal value? (See for example the discussion of this issue in Francis Fukuyama, *Our Posthuman Future: Consequences of the Biotechnology Revolution* (New York: Farrar, Straus and Giroux, 2002). Is perfection, understood as the extermination of every functional disorder, a desirable goal for human civilization? By historical experience we know that bad intentions can have good consequences, and vice versa, which adds another dimension that complicates our tasks.
48 Rita Nakashima Brock, "Losing Your Innocence But Not Your Hope," in *Reconstructing the Christ Symbol*, ed. Maryanne Stevens (New York Mahwah: Paulist Press, 1993), 43-44.

Lectures: The Challenge from Feminisms

1 Benjamin Farrington, *The Philosophy of Francis Bacon: An Essay on its Development from 1603 to 1609 with New Translations of Fundamental Texts* (Liverpool: Liverpool University Press, 1964), 18.
2 Bacon in Farrington, *Philosophy of Francis Bacon*, 63.
3 Ibid., 63.
4 Ibid., 64.
5 Ibid., 65.
6 Ibid., 66.
7 Ibid., 68.
8 Ibid., 69.

9. Ibid., 62.
10. Ibid., 72.
11. Francis Bacon, "Novum Organum," in Vol. 3 of *The Works*, edited and translated by Basil Montague (Philadelphia: Parry & MacMillan, 1854), 344, available from <http://history.hanover.edu/texts/bacon/novorg.htm> [accessed June 30, 2003].
12. Ibid., 363.
13. Georg Henrik von Wright, *Vetenskapen och förnuftet* (Stockholm: Bonniers, 1986), 65.
14. Thomas Sprat, *History of the Royal Society*, eds. Jackson I. Cope and Harold Whitmore Jones (St. Louis: Washington University Press, 1958), 327.
15. Bacon in Farrington, *Philosophy of Francis Bacon*, 62.
16. Richard Feynman, *The Development of the Space-time View of Quantum Electrodynamics*, Nobel Lecture, 1965, 155, available from <www.nobel.se/physics/laureates/1965/feynman-lecture.pdf> [accessed July 21, 2003].
17. Feynman, *Quantum Electrodynamics*, 178.
18. Carolyn Merchant, *The Death of Nature: Women, Ecology and the Scientific Revolution* (San Francisco: Harper & Row, 1989).
19. See, for example, Vandana Shiva, *Staying Alive: Women, Ecology, and Survival in India* (New Delhi: Kali for Women, 1988) and *Stolen Harvest: The Hijacking of the Global Food Supply* (Cambridge, MA: South End Press, 2000).
20. Londa Schiebinger, *The Mind Has No Sex? Women in the Origins of Modern Science* (Cambridge, MA: Harvard University Press, 1989).
21. Mary Midgley, *Evolution as a Religion: Strange Hopes and Stranger Fears* (New York and London: Methuen, 1985) and *Science as Salvation: A Modern Myth and Its Meaning* (New York and London: Routledge, 1992).
22. John Barrow, *Theories of Everything: The Quest for Ultimate Explanation* (Oxford: Clarendon, 1991), 15ff.
23. Margaret Wertheim, *Pythagoras' Trousers: God, Physics, and the Gender Wars* (New York: W.W. Norton, 1997).
24. David F. Noble, *A World Without Women: The Christian Clerical Culture of Western Science* (New York: Alfred A. Knopf, 1992) and *The Religion of Technology: The Divinity of Man and the Spirit of Invention* (New York: Penguin, 1999).
25. Vine Deloria, Jr., *Red Earth, White Lies: Native Americans and the Myth of Scientific Fact* (New York: Scribner, 1995), 17.
26. Ibid., 18.
27. Barbara A. Holmes, *Race and the Cosmos: An Invitation to View the World Differently* (Harrisburg, PA: Trinity Press International, 2002).
28. Nancy Tuana, *The Less Noble Sex: Scientific, Religious, and Philosophical Conceptions of Woman's Nature* (Bloomington: Indiana University Press, 1993), 169.
29. Ibid., xi.
30. Sharon Traweek, "Pilgrim's Progress: Male Tales Told during a Life in Physics," in *The Science Studies Reader*, ed. Mario Biagioli (New York and London: Routledge, 1999), 539. Originally published in Sharon Traweek, *Beatimes and*

Lifetimes (Cambridge: Harvard University Press, 1988 [abridged, 1998]), 74-105.
[31] Ibid.
[32] cf. also Tuana, *Less Noble Sex*, 170ff.
[33] Nancy Howell, "A Whiteheadian Case for Diversity in Science and Religion," *CTNS Bulletin* 19. 4 (1999): 7.
[34] Nancy Howell, "Science, Religion, and Women," in *Encyclopedia of Women and World Religion*, vol. 2, ed. Serinity Young (New York: Macmillan Reference USA, 1999), 873.
[35] Emily Martin, "Toward an Anthropology of Immunology: The Body as Nation State," in *The Science Studies Reader*, ed. Mario Biagioli (New York and London: Routledge, 1999), 363. Originally published in *Medical Anthropology Quarterly* 4.4 (1990).
[36] Ibid., 368.
[37] Ibid., 369.
[38] Frans de Waal, *The Ape and the Sushi Master: Cultural Reflections by a Primatologist* (New York: Basic Books, 2001) and "Without Walls," *New Scientist* 172.2321 (2001): 46ff., available from <http://groups.yahoo.com/group/evolutionary-psychology/files/dewaal.html> [accessed February 11, 2002].
[39] Sarah Blaffer Hrdy, "Raising Darwin's Consciousness: Females and Evolutionary Theory," *Zygon: Journal of Religion and Science* 25.2 (1990): 134.
[40] Quoted in Antje Jackelén, *Zeit und Ewigkeit: Die Frage der Zeit in Kirche, Naturwissenschaft und Theologie* (Neukirchen-Vluyn: Neukirchener, 2002), 211, note 211.
[41] Karen Barad, "Agential Realism: Feminist Interventions in Understanding Scientific Practices," in *The Science Studies Reader*, ed. Mario Biagioli (New York and London: Routledge, 1999), 2.
[42] Ibid., 7-8.
[43] Elizabeth A. Johnson, *She Who Is: The Mystery of God in Feminist Theological Discourse* (New York: Crossroad, 1992), 196ff., e.g.
[44] Cf. Heisenberg's line on complementarity in Michael Frayn, *Copenhagen* (London: Methuen Drama, 1998; New York: Anchor Books, 2000), 70: "I defended it at the Como Conference in 1927! I have adhered to it ever afterwards with religious fervour!"
[45] Examples of definitions according to Niels Henrik Gregersen, "Theology and the Sciences of Self-Organised Complexity," in *Evolution and Creativity: A New Dialogue Between Faith and Knowledge*, ed. C. W. du Toit (Pretoria: Research Institute for Theology and Religion, 2000), 61ff. Complex systems are systems in which there is large variability (Per Bak) or, a complex system is one in which there are more possibilities than can be actualized (Niklas Luhmann). Cf. also Niels Henrik Gregersen, ed., *From Complexity to Life: On the Emergence of Life and Meaning* (Oxford: Oxford University Press, 2003).
[46] Instead of levels, I prefer to speak of "dimensions of complexity."
[47] What is fascinating about complexity is what complexity theorists have called emergent behavior. Examples of such systems include ant colonies as well as

traffic jams and the development of neighborhoods. The organized foraging of an ant colony is determined not by the dictates of the queen but by local interactions among thousands of worker ants; neighborhoods in a modern industrial city evolve not by the dictates of a central planning board but by the independent choices made by individual people.

48 Examples: a jumbo jet, crystals or other aggregates, or a system of rational choice agents.

49 Examples: immune systems, neural systems, language systems, historically self-reflective ("Hegelian") agents. Cf. Gregersen, "Theology and the Sciences of Self-Organised Complexity," 64ff.

50 Ludwig Wittgenstein, *Tractatus Logico-Philosophicus* (New York: The Humanities Press, 1961), 11.

51 Summa Theologiae I, 1a, 3.

52 However, one could try to argue that the philosophical categories of necessity and contingency do not apply to such a system.

The Challenge from Postmodernisms

1 Mark C. Taylor, quoted in Jayne Svenungsson, *Guds återkomst: En studie av gudsbegreppet inom postmodern filosofi* (Lund: Lunds Universitet, 2002), 3.

2 Friedrich Nietzsche, *The Gay Science*, trans. Josefine Nauckhoff, ed. Bernard Williams (Cambridge: Cambridge University Press, 2001), 239-240.

3 Friedrich Nietzsche, *On the Genealogy of Morals*, trans. Walter Kaufmann and R.J. Hollingdale and *Ecce Homo*, trans. Walter Kaufmann (New York: Vintage Books, 1989), 3rd essay, section 12, 119.

4 Friedrich Nietzsche, *Götzendämmerung*, in *Sämtliche Werke: Kritische Studienausgabe, Band 6*, eds. Giorgio Colli and Mazzino Montinari (München and Berlin/New York: Deutscher Taschenbuch Verlag and Walter de Gruyter, 1980) 63. (Sprüche und Pfeile 26): "Ich misstraue allen Systematikern und gehe ihnen aus dem Weg. Der Wille zum System ist ein Mangel an Rechtschaffenheit" (my translation).

5 Rüdiger Safranski, *Nietzsche: A Philosophical Biography*, trans. Shelley Frisch (New York: W.W. Norton, 2002), 38, 48.

6 Friedrich Nietzsche, *Also sprach Zarathustra*, in *Sämtliche Werke: Kritische Studienausgabe, Band 4*, eds. Giorgio Colli and Mazzino Montinari (München and Berlin/New York: Deutscher Taschenbuch Verlag and Walter de Gruyter, 1980), 90 (my translation).

7 Friedrich Nietzsche, *The Birth of Tragedy and The Case of Wagner*, trans. Walter Kaufmann (New York: Vintage Books, 1967), section 17, 109.

8 Nietzsche, *Genealogy of Morals*, 3rd essay, section 9, 113.

9 Nietzsche, *The Birth of Tragedy*, section 17, 106.

10 Nietzsche, *The Birth of Tragedy*, section 18, 112, italics mine.

11 Nietzsche, *The Birth of Tragedy*, "Attempt at Self-Criticism," paragraph 2, 19.

[12] Friedrich Nietzsche, *Thus Spoke Zarathustra*, trans. Walter Kaufmann (New York: The Modern Library, 1995), "Prologue," paragraph 5, 17: "I say unto you: one must still have chaos in oneself to be able to give birth to a dancing star."

[13] Nietzsche, *The Birth of Tragedy*, section 18, 109.

[14] Nietzsche, *The Birth of Tragedy*, section 17, 104-109.

[15] Nietzsche, *The Birth of Tragedy*, section 15, 98.

[16] It needs to be noted that in Nietzsche "tragic" does not mean disastrous or catastrophic. Rather, in *The Birth of Tragedy*, Nietzsche refers to tragedy as the climax of culture.

[17] Nietzsche, *The Birth of Tragedy*, "Attempt at Self-Criticism," paragraph 5, 23.

[18] Friedrich Nietzsche, *Der Antichrist*, in *Sämtliche Werke: Kritische Studienausgabe, Band 6*, eds. Giorgio Colli and Mazzino Montinari (München and Berlin/New York: Deutscher Taschenbuch Verlag and Walter de Gruyter, 1980), 165-254: "Der 'Glaube' als Imperativ ist das *Veto* gegen die Wissenschaft, –*in praxi* die Lüge um jeden Preis" (225, aphorism 47). "die berühmte Geschichte ... von der Höllenangst Gottes vor der *Wissenschaft*" (226, aphorism 48).

[19] Nietzsche, *Genealogy of Morals*, 3rd essay, section 24, 151.

[20] Nietzsche, *Genealogy of Morals*, 3rd essay, section 25, 153.

[21] Nietzsche, *The Gay Science*, book 5, paragraph 381, 246.

[22] Ibid.

[23] Ibid., translation adapted by me. Original text: Friedrich Nietzsche, *Sämtliche Werke: Kritische Studienausgabe, Band 3*, eds. Giorgio Colli and Mazzino Montinari (München and Berlin/New York: Deutscher Taschenbuch Verlag and Walter de Gruyter, 1980), 635.

[24] Nietzsche, *Thus Spoke Zarathustra*, "4th and last part," paragraph 6, 260, 262.

[25] Nietzsche, *The Gay Science*, book 5, paragraph 344, 200.

[26] Friedrich Nietzsche, *Beyond Good and Evil*, translated and edited by Marion Faber (Oxford: Oxford University Press, 1998), section 1, paragraph 1, 5.

[27] Nietzsche, *The Gay Science*, book 5, paragraph 244, 200-201. (*Sämtliche Werke: Kritische Studienausgabe, Band 3*, ed. Giorgio Colli and Mazzino Montinari (München and Berlin/New York: Deutscher Taschenbuch Verlag and Walter de Gruyter, 1980), 575, 577: "Man sieht, auch die Wissenschaft ruht auf einem Glauben, es gibt gar keine 'voraussetzungslose' Wissenschaft. ... Doch man wird es begriffen haben, worauf ich hinaus will, nämlich dass es immer noch ein *metaphysischer Glaube* ist, auf dem unser Glaube an die Wissenschaft ruht,— dass auch wir Erkennenden von heute, wir Gottlosen und Antimetaphysiker, auch *unser* Feuer noch von dem Brande nehmen, den ein Jahrtausende alter Glaube entzündet hat, jener Christen-Glaube, der auch der Glaube Plato's war, dass Gott die Wahrheit ist, dass die Wahrheit göttlich ist ..."

[28] Nietzsche, *The Gay Science*, book 5, paragraph 344, 201.

[29] Karl Peters, *Dancing With the Sacred* (Harrisburg, Pennsylvania: Trinity Press International, 2002), 38.

[30] Ibid., 44.

[31] Nietzsche, *The Gay Science*, book 4, paragraph 335, 189.

32 Safranski, *Nietzsche*, 293.
33 Safranski, *Nietzsche*, 291. Compare also Heidegger who regarded Nietzsche's philosophy as the end of metaphysics.
34 Nietzsche counts idealism among the errors of his youth. He is not fond of the philosophy that grounds itself on Kant. He exclaims, for example, in *Ecce Homo*, 320: "Leibniz and Kant—these two greatest brake shoes of intellectual integrity in Europe!"
35 Nietzsche, *The Birth of Tragedy*, section 21, 130.
36 Nietzsche, *The Birth of Tragedy*, section 14, 89.
37 Bacon in Farrington, *The Philosophy of Francis Bacon*, 71.
38 John D. Caputo and Michael J. Scanlon, eds., *God, the Gift, and Postmodernism* (Bloomington and Indianapolis: Indiana University Press, 1999), 2.
39 John Caputo, *More Radical Hermeneutics* (Bloomington and Indianapolis: Indiana University Press, 2000), 154, in description of Heidegger's view of science.
40 For example, Jacques Derrida, "Circonfession: Cinquante-neuf périodes et periphrases," in *Jacques Derrida*, eds. Geoffrey Bennington and Jacques Derrida (Paris: Éditions du Seuil, 1991); Gianni Vattimo, *Credere di credere* (Milano: Garzanti, 1996); and John Caputo, *On Religion* (New York and London: Routledge, 2001). See also Svenungsson, "Att tro att man tror på en religion utan religion—om Jacques Derridas och Gianni Vattimos postmoderna bekännelser." It is an issue for discussion whether this turn to general religion [cf. also John Caputo, *The Prayers and Tears of Jacques Derrida: Religion without Religion* (Bloomington and Indianapolis: Indiana University Press, 1997)], which in some ways resembles Einstein's cosmic religiosity, is an escape from the world of historic and dogmatic particularities and contingencies into philosophical meta-religion. However, this tendency seems to be balanced by the concept of God as the indefinable "You." See also Caputo, *On Religion*, 90: "Religious transcendence is beginning to transcend the traditional religions," be it in various forms of New Age spiritualities or the mixture of mysticism and science fiction represented by, for example, *Star Wars*.
41 Emmanuel Lévinas, *Totalité et Infini: Essai sur l'extériorité* (La Haye: Martinus Nijhoff, 1961), 50ff.
42 Jean-François Lyotard, *The Postmodern Explained: Correspondence 1982-1985*, 3rd printing (Minneapolis and London: University of Minnesota Press, 1997), 12.
43 Gotthold Ephraim Lessing, "Nathan der Weise: Ein dramatisches Gedicht in fünf Aufzügen," in *Lessings Werke*, vol. 2. ed. Franz Bornmüller (Leipzig and Wien: Bibliographisches Institut, 1779). For the parable of the rings see 365ff (Dritter Aufzug, siebenter Auftritt).
44 Max Born, *My Life: Recollections of a Nobel Laureate* (London: Taylor & Francis, 1978), 298ff.
45 Caputo, *More Radical Hermeneutics*, 200.
46 Niels Bohr, *Atomteori og naturbeskrivelse* (Copenhagen: J. H. Schultz, 1958), 94. An English translation may be found in Niels Bohr, *Collected Works*, vol. 6, ed. J. Kalckar (Amsterdam, et al.: North Holland Physics Publishing, 1985), 249.

In his lecture *Atomtoerien og grundprincipperne for Naturbeskrivelsen*: "Nevertheless may we from the present state of atomic theory regard that very resignation as an essential stage in the advance of our knowledge" (my translation).

47 Emmanuel Lévinas, "La trace de l'autre," in *En découvrant l'existence avec Husserl et Heidegger* (Paris: Vrin, 1967).

48 It may be noted that what can be called a Lutheran hermeneutics, namely the emphasis on theology of the cross over against theology of glory, corresponds very well to the critique of the modern concept of sameness.

49 Lucy Tatman mentions four components of a disciplinary paradigm constituting an epistemic community: (1) a set of shared metaphysical assumptions; (2) shared metaphors; (3) shared models; (4) shared value judgments. While agreement concerning 2-4 is in principle well in the range of science-and-religion dialogue, it is precisely disagreement on the first which provides much of the dynamics of the field itself. See Lucy Tatman, *Knowledge That Matters: A Feminist Theological Paradigm and Epistemology* (Cleveland: The Pilgrim Press, 2001), 20.

50 Sergii Bulgakov, *Sophia: The Wisdom of God: An Outline of Sophiology* (Hudson, NY: Lindisfarne Press, 1993). See also Rowan Williams, ed., *Sergii Bulgakov: Towards a Russian Political Theology* (Edinburgh: T&T Clark, 1999).

51 See, for example, Vladimir Lossky, *The Mystical Theology of the Eastern Church* (Crestwood, NY: St Vladimir's Seminary Press, 1998); Paul Valliere, *Modern Russian Theology: Bukharev, Soloviev, Bulgakov* (Edinburgh: T&T Clark, 2000); and, Pavel Florensky, *The Pillar and Ground of the Truth*, trans. Boris Jakim (Princeton, NJ: Princeton University Press, 1997).

52 Jürgen Moltmann, *Science and Wisdom*, trans. Margaret Kohl (Minneapolis: Fortress, 2003).

53 Elizabeth A. Johnson, *She Who Is: The Mystery of God in Feminist Theological Discourse* (New York: Crossroad, 1992).

54 Celia E. Deane-Drummond, *Creation Through Wisdom: Theology and the New Biology* (Edinburgh: T&T Clark, 2000).

55 See Doug Oman, "A Service a Day Keeps the Doctor Away: Berkeley Study Finds Religious Attendance Prolongs Life," *Research News & Opportunities in Science and Theology* 2 (July/August 2002): 8.

56 Bacon in Farrington, *The Philosophy of Francis Bacon*, 71.

57 It is told that whenever Faraday entered his lab, he carefully locked his prayer chapel; whenever he went into his prayer room, he made sure the lab was cautiously locked. Thus he kept the two worlds he could not bring together neatly separated. See Sigurd Martin Daecke, "Gott in der Natur?" *Evangelische Kommentare* 11 (1987): 624.

Discussion Notes

[1] Sir Hamilton Alexander Roskeen Gibb, *Reflections on Islamic History and Civilization: The Complete Collected Essays of Sir Hamilton Gibb*, ed. Lawrence I. Conrad (Princeton: Darwin Press, Inc., 2002).

[2] William Montgomery Watt, author of books such as *The Formative Period of Islamic Thought* (Oxford: Oneworld Publications, 1998).

[3] Antje Jackelén, *Zeit und Ewigkeit: Die Frage der Zeit in Kirche, Naturwissenchaft und Theologie*, (Neukirchen-Vluyn: Neukirchener Verlag, 2002).

[4] Frans de Waal, *The Ape and the Sushi Master: Cultural Reflections by a Primatologist* (New York: Basic Books, 2001).

[5] Aleksandr Aleksandrovich Friedmann (Russian) found solutions to Einstein's gravitational equations (general relativity) in 1922 (Zeitschrift für Physik, 10, 37 [1922]). This solution showed that the universe began from a high density condition (singularity) and could either continue to expand or, at some time, reverse and collapse.

[6] Sergii Bulgakov, *Sophia: The Wisdom of God: An Outline of Sophiology* (Hudson, NY: Lindisfarne Press, 1993).

[7] Alexei V, Nesteruk, *Light from the East: Theology, Science, and the Eastern Orthodox Tradition* (Minneapolis: Fortress Press, 2003).

[8] This point was made succinctly by George F.R. Ellis in the second Goshen Conference on Religion and Science.

About Pandora Press

Pandora Press is a small, independently owned press dedicated to making available modestly priced books that deal with Anabaptist, Mennonite, and Believers Church topics, both historical and theological. We welcome comments from our readers.

Visit our full-service online Bookstore:
www.pandorapress.com

Ivan J. Kauffman, ed., *Just Policing: Mennonite-Catholic Theological Colloquium 2001-2002* The Bridgefolk Series (Kitchener: Pandora Press, 2004). Softcover, 127 pp., ISBN 1-894710-48-7.

Gerald W. Schlabach, ed., *On Baptism: Mennonite-Catholic Theological Colloquium 2001-2002* The Bridgefolk Series (Kitchener: Pandora Press, 2004). Softcover, 147 pp., ISBN 1-894710-47-9 ISSN 1711-9480.

Harvey L. Dyck, John R. Staples and John B. Toews, comp., trans. and ed. *Nestor Makhno and the Eichenfeld Massacre: A Civil War Tragedy in a Ukrainian Mennonite Village* (Kitchener: Pandora Press, 2004). Softcover, 115pp. ISBN 1-894710-46-0.

Jeffrey Wayne Taylor, *The Formation of the Primitive Baptist Movement* Studies in the Believers Church Tradition (Kitchener: Pandora Press, 2004). Softcover, 225 pp., includes bibliography and index. ISBN 1-894710-42-8 ISSN 1480-7432.

James C. Juhnke and Carol M. Hunter, *The Missing Peace: The Search for Nonviolent Alternatives in United States History* Second Expanded Edition (Kitchener: Pandora Press, 2004; co-published with Herald Press.) Softcover, 339 pp., includes index. ISBN 1-894710-46-3

Louise Hawkley and James C. Juhnke, eds., *Nonviolent America: History through the Eyes of Peace* Wedel Series 5 (North Newton: Bethel College, 2004, co-published with Pandora Press) Softcover, 269 pp., includes index. ISBN 1-889239-02-X

Karl Koop, *Anabaptist-Mennonite Confessions of Faith: the Development of a Tradition* (Kitchener: Pandora Press, 2004; co-published with Herald Press) Softcover, 178 pp., includes index. ISBN 1-894710-32-0

Lucille Marr, *The Transforming Power of a Century: Mennonite Central Committee and its Evolution in Ontario* (Kitchener: Pandora Press, 2003). Softcover, 390 pp., includes bibliography and index, ISBN 1-894710-41-x.

Erica Janzen, *Six Sugar Beets, Five Bitter Years* (Kitchener: Pandora Press, 2003). Softcover, 186 pp., ISBN 1-894710-37-1.

T. D. Regehr, *Faith Life and Witness in the Northwest, 1903-2003: Centenninal History of the Northwest Mennonite Conference* (Kitchener: Pandora Press, 2003). Softcover, 524 pp., includes index, ISBN 1-894710-39-8.

John A. Lapp and C. Arnold Snyder, gen.eds., *A Global Mennonite History. Volume One: Africa* (Kitchener: Pandora Press, 2003). Softcover, 320 pp., includes indexes, ISBN 1-894710-38-x.

George F. R. Ellis, *A Universe of Ethics Morality and Hope: Proceedings from the Second Annual Goshen Conference on Religion and Science* (Kitchener: Pandora Press, 2003; co-published with Herald Press.) Softcover, 148 pp. ISBN 1-894710-36-3

Donald Martin, *Old Order Mennonites of Ontario: Gelassenheit, Discipleship, Brotherhood* (Kitchener: Pandora Press, 2003; co-published with Herald Press.) Softcover, 381 pp., includes index. ISBN 1-894710-33-9

Mary A. Schiedel, *Pioneers in Ministry: Women Pastors in Ontario Mennonite Churches, 1973-2003* (Kitchener: Pandora Press, 2003) Softcover, 204 pp., ISBN 1-894710-35-5

Harry Loewen, ed., *Shepherds, Servants and Prophets* (Kitchener: Pandora Press, 2003; co-published with Herald Press) Softcover, 446 pp., ISBN 1-894710-35-5

Robert A. Riall, trans., Galen A. Peters, ed., *The Earliest Hymns of the* Ausbund: *Some Beautiful Christian Songs Composed and Sung in the Prison at Passau, Published 1564* (Kitchener: Pandora Press, 2003; co-published with Herald Press) Softcover, 468 pp., includes bibliography and index. ISBN 1-894710-34-7.

John A. Harder, *From Kleefeld With Love* (Kitchener: Pandora Press, 2003; co-published with Herald Press) Softcover, 198 pp. ISBN 1-894710-28-2

John F. Peters, *The Plain People: A Glimpse at Life Among the Old Order Mennonites of Ontario* (Kitchener: Pandora Press, 2003; co-published with Herald Press) Softcover, 54 pp. ISBN 1-894710-26-6

Robert S. Kreider, *My Early Years: An Autobiography* (Kitchener: Pandora Press, 2002; co-published with Herald Press) Softcover, 600 pp., index ISBN 1-894710-23-1

Helen Martens, *Hutterite Songs* (Kitchener: Pandora Press, 2002; co-published with Herald Press) Softcover, xxii, 328 pp. ISBN 1-894710-24-X

C. Arnold Snyder and Galen A. Peters, eds., *Reading the Anabaptist Bible: Reflections for Every Day of the Year* introduction by Arthur Paul Boers (Kitchener: Pandora Press, 2002; co-published with Herald Press.) Softcover, 415 pp. ISBN 1-894710-25-8

C. Arnold Snyder, ed., *Commoners and Community: Essays in Honour of Werner O. Packull* (Kitchener: Pandora Press, 2002; co-published with Herald Press.) Softcover, 324 pp. ISBN 1-894710-27-4

James O. Lehman, *Mennonite Tent Revivals: Howard Hammer and Myron Augsburger, 1952-1962* (Kitchener: Pandora Press, 2002; co-published with Herald Press) Softcover, xxiv, 318 pp. ISBN 1-894710-22-3

Lawrence Klippenstein and Jacob Dick, *Mennonite Alternative Service in Russia* (Kitchener: Pandora Press, 2002; co-published with Herald Press) Softcover, viii, 163 pp. ISBN 1-894710-21-5

Nancey Murphy, *Religion and Science* (Kitchener: Pandora Press, 2002; co-published with Herald Press)Softcover, 126 pp. ISBN 1-894710-20-7

Biblical Concordance of the Swiss Brethren, 1540. Trans. Gilbert Fast and Galen Peters; bib. intro. Joe Springer; ed. C. Arnold Snyder (Kitchener: Pandora Press, 2001; co-published with Herald Press) Softcover, lv, 227pp. ISBN 1-894710-16-9

Orland Gingerich, *The Amish of Canada* (Kitchener: Pandora Press, 2001; co-published with Herald Press.) Softcover, 244 pp., includes index. ISBN 1-894710-19-3

M. Darrol Bryant, *Religion in a New Key* (Kitchener: Pandora Press, 2001) Softcover, 136 pp., includes bib. refs. ISBN 1-894710- 18-5

Trans. Walter Klaassen, Frank Friesen, Werner O. Packull, ed. C. Arnold Snyder, *Sources of South German/Austrian Anabaptism* (Kitchener: Pandora Press, 2001; co-published with Herald Press.) Softcover, 430 pp. includes indexes. ISBN 1-894710-15-0

Pedro A. Sandín Fremaint y Pablo A. Jimémez, *Palabras Duras: Homilías* (Kitchener: Pandora Press, 2001). Softcover, 121 pp., ISBN 1-894710-17-7

Ruth Elizabeth Mooney, *Manual Para Crear Materiales de Educación Cristiana* (Kitchener: Pandora Press, 2001). Softcover, 206 pp., ISBN 1-894710-12-6

Esther and Malcolm Wenger, poetry by Ann Wenger, *Healing the Wounds* (Kitchener: Pandora Press, 2001; co-pub. with Herald Press). Softcover, 210 pp. ISBN 1-894710-09-6.

Otto H. Selles and Geraldine Selles-Ysselstein, *New Songs* (Kitchener: Pandora Press, 2001). Poetry and relief prints, 90pp. ISBN 1-894719-14-2

Pedro A. Sandín Fremaint, *Cuentos y Encuentros: Hacia una Educación Transformadora* (Kitchener: Pandora Press, 2001). Softcover 163 pp ISBN 1-894710-08-8.

A. James Reimer, *Mennonites and Classical Theology: Dogmatic Foundations for Christian Ethics* (Kitchener: Pandora Press, 2001; co-published with Herald Press) Softcover, 650pp. ISBN 0-9685543-7-7
Walter Klaassen, *Anabaptism: Neither Catholic nor Protestant*, 3rd ed (Kitchener: Pandora Press, 2001; co-pub. Herald Press) Softcover, 122pp. ISBN 1-894710-01-0

Dale Schrag & James Juhnke, eds., *Anabaptist Visions for the new Millennium: A search for identity* (Kitchener: Pandora Press, 2000; co-published with Herald Press) Softcover, 242 pp. ISBN 1-894710-00-2

Harry Loewen, ed., *Road to Freedom: Mennonites Escape the Land of Suffering* (Kitchener: Pandora Press, 2000; co-published with Herald Press) Hardcover, large format, 302pp. ISBN 0-9685543-5-0

Alan Kreider and Stuart Murray, eds., *Coming Home: Stories of Anabaptists in Britain and Ireland* (Kitchener: Pandora Press, 2000; co-published with Herald Press) Softcover, 220pp. ISBN 0-9685543-6-9

Edna Schroeder Thiessen and Angela Showalter, *A Life Displaced: A Mennonite Woman's Flight from War-Torn Poland* (Kitchener: Pandora Press, 2000; co-published with Herald Press) Softcover, xii, 218pp. ISBN 0-9685543-2-6

Stuart Murray, *Biblical Interpretation in the Anabaptist Tradition,* Studies in the Believers Tradition (Kitchener: Pandora Press, 2000; co-published with Herald Press) Softcover, 310pp. ISBN 0-9685543-3-4 ISSN 1480-7432.

Loren L. Johns, ed. *Apocalypticism and Millennialism,* Studies in the Believers Church Tradition (Kitchener: Pandora Press, 2000; co-published with Herald Press) Softcover, 419pp; Scripture and name indeces ISBN 0-9683462-9-4 ISSN 1480-7432

Later Writings by Pilgram Marpeck and his Circle. Volume 1: The Exposé, A Dialogue and Marpeck's Response to Caspar Schwenckfeld. Trans. Walter Klaassen, Werner Packull, and John Rempel (Kitchener: Pandora Press, 1999; co-published with Herald Press) Softcover, 157pp. ISBN 0-9683462-6-X

John Driver, *Radical Faith. An Alternative History of the Christian Church,* edited by Carrie Snyder. Kitchener: Pandora Press, 1999; co-published with Herald Press) Softcover, 334pp. ISBN 0-9683462-8-6

C. Arnold Snyder, *From Anabaptist Seed. The Historical Core of Anabaptist-Related Identity* (Kitchener: Pandora Press, 1999; co-published with Herald Press) Softcover, 53pp.; discussion questions. ISBN 0-9685543-0-X
Also available in Spanish translation: *De Semilla Anabautista,* from Pandora Press only.

John D. Thiesen, *Mennonite and Nazi? Attitudes Among Mennonite Colonists in Latin America, 1933-1945* (Kitchener: Pandora Press, 1999; co-published with Herald Press) Softcover, 330pp., 2 maps, 24 b/w illustrations, bibliography, index. ISBN 0-9683462-5-1

Lifting the Veil, a translation of *Aus meinem Leben: Erinnerungen von J.H. Janzen.* Ed. by Leonard Friesen; trans. by Walter Klaassen (Kitchener: Pandora Press, 1998; co-pub. with Herald Press). Softcover, 128pp.; 4pp. of illustrations. ISBN 0-9683462-1-9

Leonard Gross, *The Golden Years of the Hutterites*, rev. ed. (Kitchener: Pandora Press, 1998; co-pub. with Herald Press). Softcover, 280pp., index. ISBN 0-9683462-3-5

William H. Brackney, ed., *The Believers Church: A Voluntary Church*, Studies in the Believers Church Tradition (Kitchener: Pandora Press, 1998; co-published with Herald Press). Softcover, viii, 237pp., index. ISBN 0-9683462-0-0 ISSN 1480-7432.

An Annotated Hutterite Bibliography, compiled by Maria H. Krisztinkovich, ed. by Peter C. Erb (Kitchener: Pandora Press, 1998). (Ca. 2,700 entries) 312pp., cerlox bound, electronic, or both. ISBN (paper) 0-9698762-8-9/(disk) 0-9698762-9-7

Jacobus ten Doornkaat Koolman, *Dirk Philips. Friend and Colleague of Menno Simons*, trans. W. E. Keeney, ed. C. A. Snyder (Kitchener: Pandora Press, 1998; co-published with Herald Press). Softcover, xviii, 236pp., index. ISBN: 0-9698762-3-8

Sarah Dyck, ed./tr., *The Silence Echoes: Memoirs of Trauma & Tears* (Kitchener: Pandora Press, 1997; co-published with Herald Press). Softcover, xii, 236pp., 2 maps. ISBN: 0-9698762-7-0

Wes Harrison, *Andreas Ehrenpreis and Hutterite Faith and Practice* (Kitchener: Pandora Press, 1997; co-published with Herald Press). Softcover, xxiv, 274pp., 2 maps, index. ISBN 0-9698762-6-2

C. Arnold Snyder, *Anabaptist History and Theology: Revised Student Edition* (Kitchener: Pandora Press, 1997; co-pub. Herald Press). Softcover, xiv, 466pp., 7 maps, 28 illustrations, index, bibliography. ISBN 0-9698762-5-4

Nancey Murphy, *Reconciling Theology and Science: A Radical Reformation Perspective* (Kitchener, Ont.: Pandora Press, 1997; co-pub. Herald Press). Softcover, x, 103pp., index. ISBN 0-9698762-4-6

C. Arnold Snyder and Linda A. Huebert Hecht, eds, *Profiles of Anabaptist Women: Sixteenth Century Reforming Pioneers* (Waterloo, Ont.: Wilfrid Laurier University Press, 1996). Softcover, xxii, 442pp. ISBN: 0-88920-277-X

The Limits of Perfection: A Conversation with J. Lawrence Burkholder 2nd ed., with a new epilogue by J. Lawrence Burkholder, Rodney Sawatsky and Scott Holland, eds. (Kitchener: Pandora Press, 1996). Softcover, x, 154pp. ISBN 0-9698762-2-X

C. Arnold Snyder, *Anabaptist History and Theology: An Introduction* (Kitchener: Pandora Press, 1995). ISBN 0-9698762-0-3 Softcover, x, 434pp., 6 maps, 29 illustrations, index,bibliography.

Pandora Press
33 Kent Avenue
Kitchener, ON N2G 3R2
CANADA
Tel.: (519) 578-2381 / Fax: (519) 578-1826
E-mail: info@pandorapress.com
Web site: www.pandorapress.com